Acknowledgments

Many puzzle inventors and enthusiasts have helped me in this project by letting me use their puzzle designs, providing background information on puzzles, and offering comments and suggestions. My gratitude goes to Stewart Coffin, Bob Easter, Harry Eng, Christiaan Freeling, Rick Irby, Scott Kim, Harry Nelson, Gene Novak, Jerry Slocum, Howard Swift, Anneke Treep, and Nob Yoshigahara. I feel indebted to math educator Claudia Zaslavsky and mathematicians Elwyn Berlekamp and James King, authorities in their academic fields, who have given me much needed guidance and support.

Stan Isaacs of Palo Alto, California, gave tremendous support to this project. In fact, it was his puzzle party at the 1993 Summer Institute of Key Curriculum Press that rekindled my childhood passion for puzzles and led to my writing this book. Thank you, Stan.

Many thanks to all the teachers, educators, and students who attended my puzzle workshops and made puzzles, especially to the teachers Catherine Reinke, Lee Tempkin, Ada Wada, and Gloria Wong and their classes. Family and friends both in the United States and in China showed their support by becoming testers of the puzzles, critics of the manuscript, and assistants at my puzzle workshops. Thank you all, and I love you.

Special thanks to Peter Rasmussen, without whose encouragement and support this book would not have been possible. Peter was the first to listen to my ideas, read my writing, and try out some of the puzzles I made. He also edited the manuscript so many times and did so much of the research with me that he is really a coauthor of this book.

I'd like to thank Joe Todaro, my editor at Key Curriculum Press, who gave me many suggestions for improvements and whose professional help has enhanced this book in many ways.

Finally, my thanks to Key Curriculum Press and its staff for their confidence and support in this project and for giving me this opportunity to do what I enjoy doing.

Wei Zhang

About the Author

Wei Zhang was born in Urumqi, the capital of Xinjiang Province in China. As a child, her favorite book was *The Moscow Puzzles* by Boris Kordemsky. When she was 11 years old, she saw the *Chinese Rings* puzzle for the first time and immediately fell in love with it.

Wei came to North America in 1983 for her education and training in linguistics and computer science. However, she finds it far more intriguing to roam in the world of mechanical puzzles. Once in a while she writes a computer program to prove or confirm her puzzle conjectures.

Wei enjoys traveling, cooking, gardening, and opera in addition to making puzzles at her workbench.

Exploring Math Through Puzzles

Blackline Masters for Making over 50 Puzzles

Wei Zhang

KEY CURRICULUM PRESS
Innovators in Mathematics Education

MATHEMATICS DEPARTMENT
ALVERNO COLLEGE
MILWAUKEE, WI 53234-3922

Limited Reproduction Permission

Key Curriculum Press grants the teacher who purchases *Exploring Math Through Puzzles* the right to reproduce the puzzle instruction and activity pages for use in his or her own classroom.

Unauthorized copying of *Exploring Math Through Puzzles*, however, constitutes copyright infringement and is a violation of federal law.

Camera-ready copy supplied by the author.

10 9 8 7 6 5 4 3   01 00 99 98

Published by Key Curriculum Press, 1150 65th Street, Emeryville, California 94608

email: editorial@keypress.com
http://www.keypress.com

Printed in the United States of America.   ISBN 1-55953-222-X

Table of Contents

Puzzles

Preface

Exploring Math Through Puzzles is a book on puzzles. It also explores some of the mathematics that can be learned through puzzle-making and puzzle-solving activities. The 54 puzzles included in the book have been selected because they illustrate various mathematical principles. Although this book was written to be used in grades 5 through 12 math classrooms, it is also intended for anyone outside the classroom who is interested in puzzles. I hope *Exploring Math Through Puzzles* will play a constructive role in math education—both in the classroom and at home.

Exploring Math Through Puzzles is divided into three main parts: the mathematics of the puzzles, puzzle-making techniques and skills, and instructions for making 54 puzzles. The mathematical section discusses some of the mathematical principles on which the puzzles are based and suggests classroom explorations and investigations related to the puzzles. The techniques and skills section offers practical suggestions and tips to those about to begin making their own puzzles. Finally, there is a one-page instruction sheet for each of the 54 puzzles.

Each instruction sheet contains a brief introduction to the puzzle, a list of required materials, an illustration of the puzzle in its initial state, step-by-step instructions telling how to make the puzzle, and the objective (or final state) to be reached in solving it. Some pages feature an optional "Stop and Play" section, which highlights a suggestion on how the puzzle-maker can pause to explore the puzzle before completing it. Other pages feature a "Variations" section containing suggestions on how to make related puzzles.

The difficulty level of each puzzle is indicated by two dice. One die notes the difficulty in making the puzzle and the other notes the difficulty in solving it. The difficulty levels range from one (easy) to six (hard). A die of ⚃ indicates a difficulty level of four (somewhat difficult). Most of these puzzles are easy to construct and solve. Some of them are especially designed for young puzzle-makers and beginners. Do make some, if not all, of the puzzles—and have fun solving them!

Happy puzzling!

Wei Zhang

Introduction

Puzzles are problems done for fun. They are a form of entertainment, but also a form of exercise—a way to get your mind into shape. A mechanical puzzle, one that involves physical manipulation of one or more pieces, also satisfies an inborn desire to fidget. With a mechanical puzzle, you have something to keep your hands occupied while you are thinking about a solution. It tends to be involving even for people who don't normally like puzzles.

This is a book about making mechanical puzzles. As a long time devotee of puzzles, and a collector of mechanical puzzles for the last couple of decades, I am excited that we now have access to many types of puzzles at a moderate price.

This book was developed by Wei Zhang for classroom use. Why would you use puzzles in a classroom? Aren't they just a waste of time, a way to keep students quiet and occupied for a while? I believe they can be used in a more constructive manner. They can excite students, stimulate thought, point to research, and involve students in their own educational process. Puzzles can help make learning fun!

It is clear that puzzles can be useful for gifted students, as a way of giving them more advanced projects. But they are actually useful for *all* students. They seem to grab people's attention in a way few things do. The physical nature of mechanical puzzles fascinates many types of people, and can be more involving than listening to a lecture and passive watching.

A puzzle is a challenge, but should still be fun. There is an important distinction to be made between "challenging" and "frustrating"—and a teacher needs to be prepared to try to walk that line. Offering hints to the students might help. Alternatively, approaching puzzle "problems" as a sequence building in complexity may be useful. Choose a sequence of puzzles carefully, so each introduces a new concept as well as builds on previous ones.

Several puzzles can be seen as variations on a theme. A single puzzle idea can be realized in a large variety of forms, or a single form of a puzzle can hide many different problems. With this puzzle kit, one can explore some of these variations. Try fewer cubes, different colors, a wire shaped as a school insignia—variations can make a puzzle easier, harder, or more attractive, or give it some special relevance.

A puzzle is a problem that is solved for the sake of finding a solution—not to get a grade, nor to make money, nor even to please a boss. Many scientists and mathematicians like their work so much because they treat every problem they encounter as a puzzle to be solved. It's fun! They don't solve problems because it's their job, they choose the job because it allows them to spend their time solving puzzles.

But this is more than just a puzzle book. The book includes material on how to make the puzzles, suggestions about how to use them in a classroom, the mathematical concepts involved, some puzzle history and puzzle classification, hints of solutions, and much more. Using puzzles to teach thinking and problem solving can be fun and economical. And remember, a puzzle is worth a thousand problems.

Stanley Isaacs

Palo Alto, California

Puzzles and the Math Classroom

Puzzles in the math classroom? What do puzzles have to do with teaching mathematics? How can puzzles be used in the math classroom? These are a few of the questions this section tries to answer.

Puzzles and Mathematics

Puzzles

Puzzles, in general, are problems that invite solutions. In this book, the term *puzzle* is used to refer only to mechanical puzzles and does not include crossword puzzles, brain teasers, and the like.

A puzzle is a manufactured object or collection of objects that one can hold and play with. It is solved through manipulation by using one's intelligence and dexterity, or by just plain luck. Puzzles are sometimes classified as games. If you go to a bookstore, you will probably find puzzle books in the games section. And like most games, a puzzle consists of the following four essentials:

1. An object that one can play with
2. An initial state (or configuration) of the object
3. A set of rules for manipulation of the object, and
4. A final state of the object

When you have a puzzle, the final state is the solution to the puzzle.

Mathematics

Mathematics is a way of thinking. The teaching of mathematics is not simply showing what and how, but, most importantly, why. Looking at the mathematics curriculum of schools (grades 5 through 12), one can always find algebra and geometry. However, no one can really learn algebra and geometry without developing an understanding of the principles underlying these disciplines. Mathematics in the classroom, therefore, should include the development of logical reasoning and spatial thinking in addition to the basic mathematical skills.

What Do Puzzles and Mathematics Have in Common?

A lot of puzzles are physical embodiments of mathematical problems. Because of this one can often apply mathematical principles in the solution of puzzles. Sometimes the solution to one puzzle relies on the application of several different mathematical principles.

Why Use Puzzles in the Math Classroom?

Classrooms are places of learning. Math classrooms should be places where mathematical explorations and discoveries are made by inquisitive minds. Any manipulative that facilitates such activities should find a place in the math classroom. Puzzles that embody mathematical problems belong in the math classroom for two reasons. First, constructing such puzzles can lead to the discovery and better understanding of mathematical principles. And secondly, solving such puzzles helps students to develop many of the same skills learned in other math problems, and has the additional advantage of being a hands-on activity.

Puzzles Are Fun

People treat puzzles as toys. It is a lot easier to get people involved in "puzzle playing" than in "abstract mathematical learning." Puzzles can be used to entice students to learn while "playing." The properties of many branches of mathematics, such as geometry, graph theory, and topology, can be demonstrated using puzzle examples. With such hands-on experience, playing with puzzles can lead to "inquisitive learning," and students can make their own discoveries in math as opposed to just being fed mathematical principles.

Puzzles Are a Form of Problem Solving

Like other math problems, puzzles are meant to be solved. Finding solutions to puzzles calls for an understanding of the mathematical principles behind the puzzles. In addition, the process of solving puzzles helps students develop and enhance their problem-solving skills. The use of puzzles in the math classroom can also help students develop their analytical skills, logical reasoning, and understanding of spatial relationships.

Puzzle Making Is a Constructive Activity

For each puzzle in this book there is a list of materials required and a set of instructions for its construction. In making these puzzles, students must read the instructions and follow the steps and figures. In addition, they are provided with an opportunity to use their hands and their brains at the same time.

The Mathematics of Puzzles

Puzzles are manipulatives that can add fun and creativity to the classroom. Just like any other teaching aid, puzzles themselves do not facilitate learning unless they are used in a constructive way. In this section we suggest some math-related activities for each group of puzzles.

The puzzles in this book were carefully selected to motivate students to think about a wide range of mathematical topics. Although some of the topics, such as topology, may not be part of the curriculum in every school, a brief introduction to these topics through puzzle solving will broaden the students' scope of learning and enhance their ways of thinking and reasoning.

Cube Construction Puzzles

Four of the puzzles in this book involve the construction of cubes out of smaller pieces. In each of these puzzles, 27 small cubes, called unit cubes, are used to form several geometric pieces, each of which is made up of two or more cubes glued together face to face. The objective of each puzzle is to put these geometric pieces together to form a 3 × 3 × 3 cube.

Geometric Properties of the Cube Pieces

When two or more unit cubes are glued together face to face, they form a **polycube**. For ease of reference and identification, each polycube piece is labeled with two numbers separated by a hyphen. The first number indicates how many unit cubes were used to make up the piece, and the second number indicates the arbitrary placement of this piece in a sequence of polycubes all made of the same number of cubes.

There is only one way of forming a piece out of two cubes, and there are two ways of forming a piece out of three cubes. The two- and three-cube pieces are shown below along with their labels.

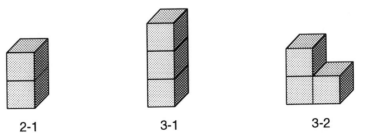

2-1   3-1   3-2

A polycube has certain special properties determined by its shape. A polycube is **flat** if all its cubes can lie flat on the same plane. All two- and three-cube polycubes are flat.

A polycube has **reflexive symmetry** if it can be divided into two equal parts by an imaginary plane (horizontally, vertically, or diagonally) so that the two parts are mirror images of each other. This imaginary plane is called a **plane of symmetry**. Some of the polycubes have more than one plane of symmetry. All two- and three-cube pieces have reflexive symmetry. It is easy to find planes of symmetry in polycubes 2-1 and 3-1. How about 3-2? Can you find its two planes of symmetry?

In fact, all flat polycubes have reflexive symmetry. That is because you can always divide any flat piece by an imaginary plane passing through the center of its thickness and get two identical halves that are mirror images of each other. To see this, imagine that piece 4-2 below is made of cheese and is cut into two equal slices through its thickness. If the top slice were to flip over and lie flat next to the other slice, you would see that they are mirror images of each other.

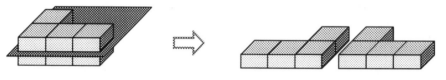

Combinatorial Geometry

Putting unit geometric shapes together to form more complex geometric pieces is an activity of **combinatorial geometry**. Combinatorial geometry is the study of geometric arrangements, permutations, combinations, and enumerations of geometric patterns. Our patterns here are formed by unit cubes, and we will explore how the unit cubes can be put together (arranged) and the properties of their constructions. In the constructions, the unit cubes can only be put together face to face.

Students will learn about the combinatorial geometry of cubes while constructing polycube pieces. The *Diabolical Cube* is made out of flat pieces only, while the *Half-Hour Cube* is made only out of nonflat pieces. The *Soma Cube* and *Nob's Cube* are made out of both flat and nonflat pieces.

There are a total of eight polycubes that can be built out of four unit cubes. As you can see, five of these polycube pieces are flat and three are nonflat. The five flat pieces and one of the nonflat pieces are reflexively symmetric.

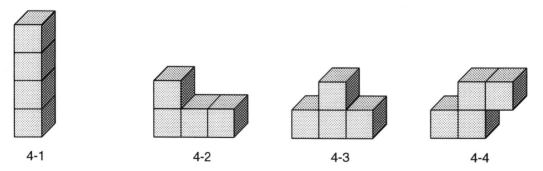

4-1   4-2   4-3   4-4

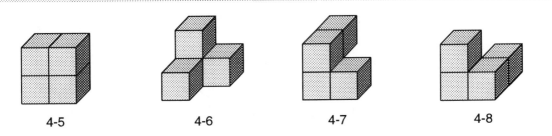

4-5 4-6 4-7 4-8

The pieces that form the *Soma Cube* consist of all the nonrectangular polycubes that can be made out of three or four unit cubes. Can you identify all the pieces? The *Soma Cube* is the most famous of the cube construction puzzles. In addition to the 240 different ways of putting the pieces together to form a 3 × 3 × 3 cube, you can also use them to construct many other interesting shapes, such as those shown below. (See Activity 5— *Soma Cube* Constructions, on page 104.)

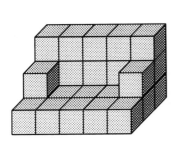 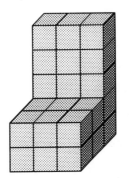 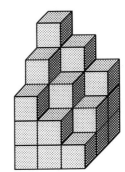

There are 29 ways to make five-cube polycubes, 12 of which are flat. The 12 flat five-cube polycubes are called **solid pentominoes** (as in *dominoes*). The word **pentomino** comes from **polyomino,** which was coined in 1953 by Professor Solomon W. Golomb in his research on the combinatorial geometry of connected squares.

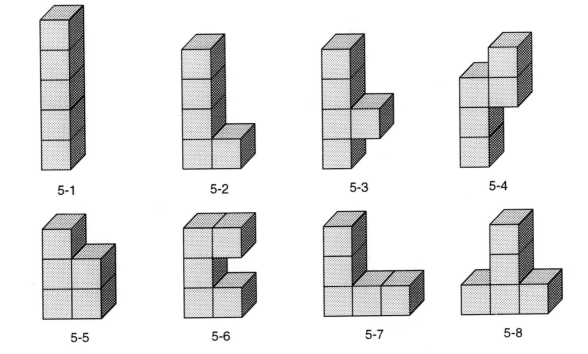

5-1 5-2 5-3 5-4

5-5 5-6 5-7 5-8

Exploring Math Through Puzzles

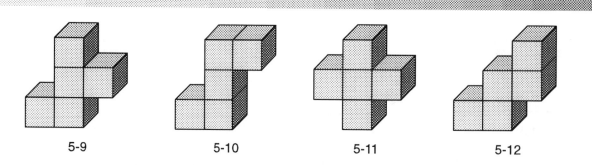

5-9   5-10   5-11   5-12

The 12 solid pentominoes form a fascinating puzzle that is sold in many game stores. Each pentomino has been given one of the following alphabetic names: F, I, L, P, S, T, U, V, W, X, Y, and Z. Can you match each pentomino with its alphabetic name? Some of them require a little imagination. The alphabetic names provide a more interesting way of referring to the pieces than the number combinations—and they're easier to remember, too!

A classical pentomino problem is to use all 12 pieces to make a checkerboard with a 2×2 square hole in its center. Not counting differences due to rotation and reflection, there are 65 different solutions! You can find references to the pentomino checkerboard problem in many puzzle books.

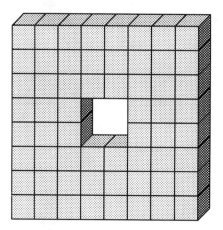

Another challenge is to pack the 12 solid pentominoes into the following solid rectangular shapes: $2 \times 3 \times 10$, $2 \times 5 \times 6$, and $3 \times 4 \times 5$. Pentominoes can also be used to construct many other interesting and challenging shapes. The pyramid below left uses only 11 pieces, while the staircase on the right uses all 12 pentominoes.

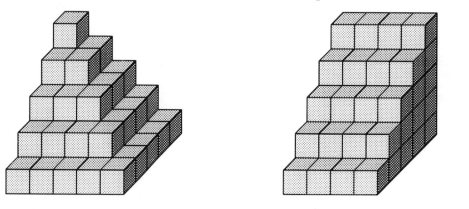

In addition to the 12 pentominoes, there are 17 nonflat polycubes made of five cubes. The nonflat pieces are an interesting group, too. Each piece is either reflexively symmetric or a mirror image of another piece. Can you identify the pieces that have reflexive symmetry? Can you match the pieces that are mirror images of each other?

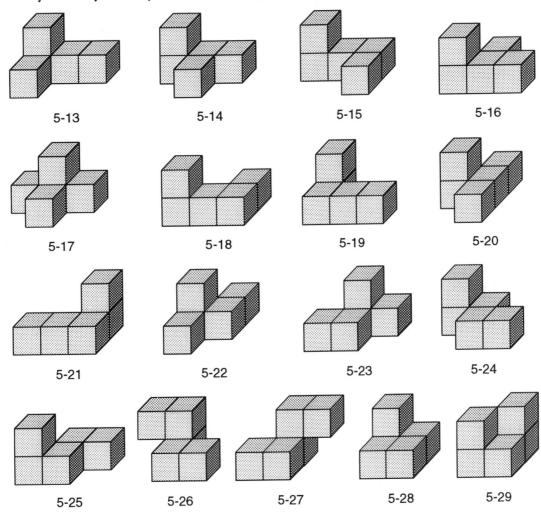

5-13   5-14   5-15   5-16

5-17   5-18   5-19   5-20

5-21   5-22   5-23   5-24

5-25   5-26   5-27   5-28   5-29

See Activity 4—Polycubes, on page 103, for a set of challenging questions about polycube structures and properties.

Exploring Math Through Puzzles

Object Orientation Puzzles

An **object orientation** puzzle is made up of a set of objects that are identical in shape, but different in surface design (color, texture, or graphics). To solve the puzzle you have to arrange and orient the objects so that they satisfy some defined objective. *Instant Insanity* and *Bewitching Cubes* are object orientation puzzles. Each consists of a set of cubes with different colors on their six faces. There are many interesting mathematical explorations associated with such sets of cubes.

The Layouts of a Cube

How can we cut out a piece of paper so that it can be folded into a cube with no overlapping faces? We know that a cube has six faces which are equal-sized squares, so one way would be to cut out six squares that are connected edge to edge and fold the cut out pattern along the common edges of the squares to form a cube. We'll call this kind of pattern a **layout** of a cube.

A five-square construction is called a pentomino, so what do you suppose a six-square construction is called? It is a **hexomino**, of course. There are 35 ways of connecting six equal-sized squares together edge to edge. But not all 35 hexominoes can be folded into a cube. For example, neither the 1 × 6 nor the 2 × 3 hexomino can be folded into a cube. In addition, no hexomino that has a 2 × 2 square as part of it will fold into a cube. What other types of hexominoes cannot be folded into cubes?

Following are the 11 hexominoes that can be folded into a cube. These are all the layouts of a cube.

The Color Configurations of a Cube

A cube has six faces. If we have six colors and color each face with a different color, how many different ways can we color the cube? To help answer this question, let's record the colors of the cube's faces on a †-shaped layout. The color of each face is recorded in one of the squares, as shown below.

Let's choose colors for the back, top, front, bottom, left, and right faces, in that order. To start with, we have six colors to choose from for the back face of the cube. And since the top face must be a different color from the back face, there are five color choices left for the top face. And, likewise, since the front face must be a different color from both the back and the top faces, there are four color choices left for the front face. Continuing in this way, we can figure out the total number of different ways of coloring the six faces of the cube: $6 \times 5 \times 4 \times 3 \times 2 \times 1 = 720$.

But wait a minute! Are there any duplicates among these 720 descriptions? The figure in the center above shows one of the colored cubes in the *Bewitching Cubes* puzzle. But the figure on the right above shows the same cube rotated 90° clockwise around the top face. So for each color configuration of a cube, there are some duplicate descriptions—but how many?

This question is the same as asking how many different descriptions represent the same color configuration of a cube. Well, imagine we have a cube with six different colors on the six faces. Now we want to describe this cube by plotting the six colors on †-shaped layouts. For each description we can choose one of the six colors as the top face color, and for each color chosen as the top face, we can choose one of the four side face colors as the front face. In other words, a cube has six faces and for each face we can have four rotations, therefore we have $4 \times 6 = 24$ different ways to describe each color configuration. (See Activity 6—Describing a Cube, on page 105.)

Given the above, it follows that the number of different ways a cube can be colored with six different colors is $720 \div 24 = 30$.

Here is a question for the class: What are the 30 different ways of coloring the six faces of a cube with six different colors?

Using Graph Representations to Solve Object Orientation Puzzles

As mentioned earlier, *Instant Insanity* is a puzzle of object orientation. It consists of four cubes, and the sides of the cubes are colored with four different colors—Red, Green, Blue, and Yellow. The following are the layout plans of the four cubes:

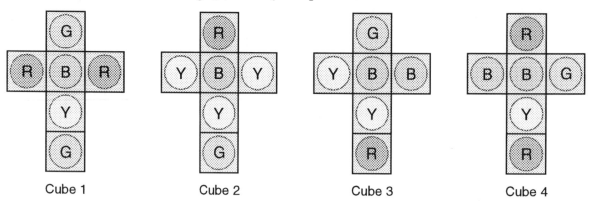

Cube 1   Cube 2   Cube 3   Cube 4

The objective of the puzzle is to arrange the cubes in a row so that all four colors appear on each of the row's four sides.

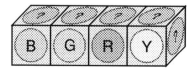

Considering the fact that the ordering of the cubes plays no role in the solution of the puzzle, how many different ways can we arrange the four cubes in a row? Let's find out first how many different ways there are to arrange the first cube. Each cube has six faces that form three opposite pairs, front-back, top-bottom, and left-right. Since one pair of opposite faces will not be involved as faces of the row in each arrangement, there is a total of three ways to arrange the first cube. Once the first cube is positioned, the second, third, and fourth cubes each has 24 arrangements. That's because for each of the cube's six faces there are four rotations. Thus, there are $3 \times 24 \times 24 \times 24 = 41,472$ different ways of arranging the four cubes in a row. It looks hopelessly impractical to use the trial-and-error approach to solve this puzzle.

Using graph representations, however, we can solve the puzzle quite efficiently. In a graph, there are dots and lines linking the dots. The dots are called **nodes** and the lines are called **edges**. First let's represent each cube by a graph of the opposite-faced pairs. We use the four colors as nodes and link the nodes of each pair of opposite faces with an edge. If a pair of opposite faces has the same color, then we draw a loop connecting the node to itself. Since each cube has three pairs of opposite faces, the graph representation for each cube has three edges linking the four color nodes. For easy reference, the four graphs of the cubes of *Instant Insanity* are numbered in the order in which they appear above.

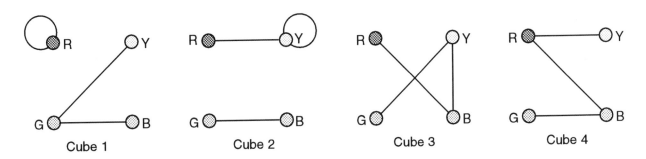

Cube 1   Cube 2   Cube 3   Cube 4

Now let's combine the four graphs into one by using one set of the color nodes and superimposing all the edges. The combined graph has four nodes and 12 edges, and each edge is labeled with the number of the cube it is associated with.

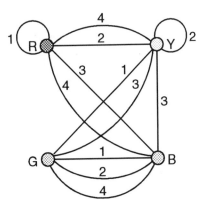

In the combined graph above, the 12 edges show the color relationship of the 12 pairs of opposite faces of the puzzle's four cubes. Since the solution of the puzzle requires that the cubes be arranged in a row, eight of the 12 edges will give us the information of the colors of each of the row's four sides. If the puzzle has a solution—and we know it does—then we should be able to find the eight edges that can help us arrange the cubes so that all four colors appear on each of the row's four sides. Four of the eight edges show the row's top and bottom colors and the other four show the row's front and back colors.

To find the eight edges, we need to extract two subgraphs of four nodes and four edges from the combined graph. Each subgraph must have an edge from each of the four cubes and the two subgraphs must have no edge in common. In addition, each node in the subgraph either must be looped with an edge or linked with two edges. Finding the subgraphs takes some thinking, but it is not very difficult.

Exploring Math Through Puzzles   13

Since each of the subgraphs represents the color relationship of a pair of opposite-faced sides, let's see how we can use the subgraphs to solve the puzzle. First, we use the subgraph on the left for the row's top and bottom sides. Starting with the first cube, we can position it with yellow on top and green on bottom. Following the edge, the second cube has to be positioned with green on top and blue on bottom, the third cube has blue and red, and the fourth cube has red and yellow. Now the top and bottom sides have all four colors, but this is not necessarily true for the front and back sides. Following the edges in the subgraph on the right, we can arrange the colors of the front and back faces of the cubes by rotating them around the top face. If the first cube has green-blue for its front and back, then, following the edges, the fourth cube has to have blue-red for its front and back, and the second and third cubes have red-yellow and yellow-green for their front and back colors. Here we have the solution to *Instant Insanity*.

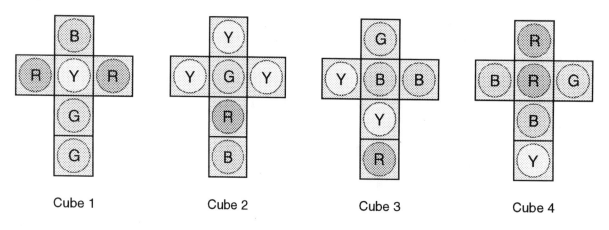

| Cube 1 | Cube 2 | Cube 3 | Cube 4 |

The following is a list of questions that can help you in understanding the graph representations of the puzzle and in using this approach to solve an object orientation puzzle. (Also see Activity 7—Graph Representations, on page 106.)

1. In the graphs, does it matter what colors the nodes are labeled? For example, if we exchange the labels of red with blue in the graph for cube 1 and link the nodes with edges of opposite colors, can we still get the same graph?
2. When extracting two subgraphs from the combined graph, how do you select edges for the subgraphs or eliminate edges from them? Explain why the loop edge of cube 1 around node R cannot be used in a subgraph.

3. We used the subgraph on the left for the top and bottom faces of the solution of the puzzle. Would it still work if we used the subgraph for the front and back faces? Explain why.

4. Why is it important to follow the edges when using a subgraph to arrange the cubes? If we choose green-yellow in the subgraph on the left for the first cube's top and bottom colors, how do you arrange the rest of the cubes for their top and bottom faces?

5. Can you design a puzzle with four cubes and four colors that has no solution? What is the key in such a design?

6. We know from the graph representations that *Instant Insanity* has only one solution. Remember, the ordering of the cubes and the rotation of the row are not considered significant in the puzzle's solution. Can you modify this puzzle so that it will have two or more solutions? What is the key to a multiple-solution puzzle of this kind?

Now that you know how to solve *Instant Insanity* using graph representations, can you solve the puzzle *Bewitching Cubes*? It consists of six cubes, and there are six different colors on the six faces of each cube.

Puzzles and Topology

Topology is the study of geometric properties that are preserved under deformation. Sometimes topology is referred to as "rubber sheet geometry." Topologically speaking, there is no difference between a doughnut and a coffee cup, since either one can be deformed into the shape of the other. Many string and wire puzzles are based on topological principles. Understanding a few basic principles will help you analyze and solve these puzzles.

Open Loop Puzzles

The lock puzzles, the clef puzzles, and the *Chinese Rings* puzzle are based on the **open loop** principle. An open loop is a loop structure that has one or more openings. An open loop puzzle consists of at least two parts, including an open loop and a second loop (either another open loop or a **closed loop**) structured so that it can pass through the opening(s) of the open loop. Initially these two parts are interlocked, and the objective of the puzzle is to separate them.

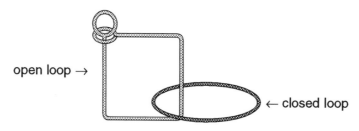

open loop →   ← closed loop

Simple Open Loop Puzzles

In each puzzle shown below, a length of wire and a bead are used to form an open loop. One end of the wire is attached to a bead, and the other end is bent into a small circle that we call an **end loop**. The end loop holds the other end of the wire inside itself, and therefore it is also called a **locking loop**. Since the bead at the end of the wire is too large to pass through the locking loop, an open loop structure is formed in the wire. Interlocked with each open loop is a closed loop made of string. Topologically, an open loop is not really a loop at all. To see this, just imagine "shrinking" the bead at the end of the wire until it is very small. Then pass it through the locking loop. Once you've done that, the loop that was interlocked with the string no longer exists.

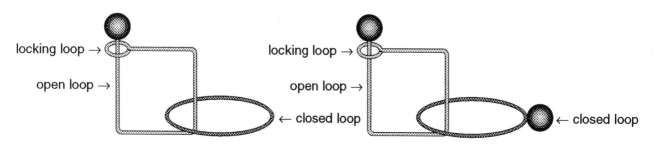

locking loop →   locking loop →

open loop →   open loop →

← closed loop   ← closed loop

In every puzzle based on the open loop principle, it appears that the two loops are inextricably interlocked. However, once we recognize an open loop structure in a puzzle, we can always find a way for the interlocked object to pass through the opening of the open loop. In the first puzzle, we can push the string through the locking loop and it is off. But how do we solve the second puzzle? The second puzzle has a string loop with a bead threaded on it, and the bead is too large to pass through the locking loop. Let's try to push the string loop through the locking loop just far enough to let it pass over the bead attached to the end of the wire and then pull the string back through the locking loop. It works, and the string loop is free!

So far we have only looked at open loop puzzles in which the locked objects are string loops. Strings are flexible and can be twisted and folded at will, so once we figure out where the opening is in the open loop structure, getting the locked string loop out is easy. In this book we have several open loop puzzles that are made completely out of wire. In a wire puzzle all parts have fixed shapes that cannot be changed. How do we solve these wire open loop puzzles?

The *Heart Lock* puzzle shown below is a wire open loop puzzle. The square is an open loop because there is an opening at the ends of the wire. Interlocked with the square is a heart, which is a closed loop because the ends of the wire are tightly locked together with no opening. How do we separate the heart and the square?

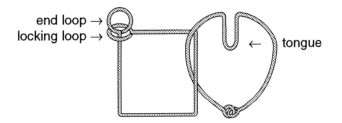

We know that it is impossible for the heart to pass completely through the square's locking loop, as in our first string loop example, because the heart is much too big. Now let's see if we can push the heart partially through the locking loop and pass it over the end loop, as in our second string loop example. First of all, we have to find a part of the heart that's narrow enough to slide into the square's locking loop. Secondly, we have to make sure that this part is long enough to pass over the end loop. The long, narrow part of the heart that allows us to separate it from the square is called a **tongue**.

Using this strategy, we can solve *Heart Lock* in three steps:
1. Hold the heart upside down and pull the tongue into the locking loop from inside the square;
2. Pass the tip of the tongue over the end loop; and
3. Push the tongue out of the locking loop to free the heart.

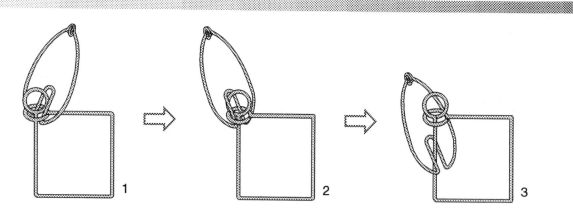

Now we know how to free a closed loop from an open loop in a simple open loop puzzle. To interlock them again, we follow the same steps in reverse. When an open loop puzzle is made completely of rigid material like wire, always look for the opening(s) in the open loop part of the puzzle and the tongue in the other loop of the puzzle.

Transforming Open Loop Puzzles

Some puzzles, such as *Double Treble Clef* and other clef puzzles, have quite complicated designs. When solving a topological puzzle with a complicated structure, the first thing to do is simplify the structure. One way to do this is by reducing the number of **crossings**. *Crossing* is a term used in knot theory (a branch of topology) to refer to a point where two segments of a knot meet and one segment passes over the other segment.

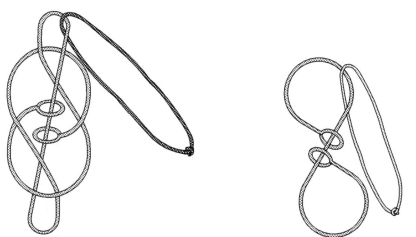

Let's use the *Double Treble Clef* and *Figure 8* puzzles as an example. The *Figure 8* puzzle on the right has two open loops sharing one piece of wire. Each open loop also functions as the end loop for the other open loop. There are no crossings in the puzzle, and the entrance to each open loop is in the center of the wire between the two locking loops. *Figure 8* is a rather simple puzzle to solve. On the other hand, *Double Treble Clef*, with its eight crossings, appears to be a difficult puzzle. However, if you examine its structure closely, you'll see that *Double Treble Clef* is not very different from *Figure 8*.

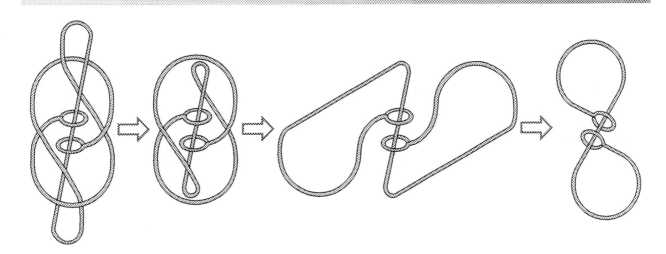

The figures above show a series of "rubber wire" transformations that change *Double Treble Clef* into *Figure 8*. Notice how the eight crossings disappear as the clef is untangled. Can you solve *Double Treble Clef* now?

Nested Open Loops

Open loop structures can be nested to form more complicated puzzles. *Double Trapeze* and *Chinese Rings* are typical nested open loop puzzles. When we have a nested open loop structure, it is important to be able to see the structure of each individual open loop, where the openings are, and how the loops are nested together.

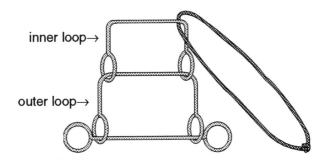

inner loop→

outer loop→

The *Double Trapeze* puzzle has two open loops nested together. The openings of both open loops are the end loops in their U-shaped structure. The openings of the inner loop lead to the outer loop, and the openings of the outer loop lead outside the whole puzzle. To free the string loop from the puzzle, we first move it from the inner loop to the outer loop and then move it outside the outer loop. Why not make this puzzle and try it out by following the steps below to free the string loop?

1. Push part of the string loop through one of the locking loops from inside the inner loop.
2. Interlock with the outer loop the part of the string loop that has been pushed through the locking loop. This is just like interlocking a string loop with a simple open loop. Be careful not to make any crossings in the string loop.

Exploring Math Through Puzzles

3. Pull the string back out of the locking loop. Now the string loop should be interlocked with the outer loop only.

4. Remove the string loop from the outer loop in the same way that you solve a simple open loop puzzle. Now the string loop should be free.

We can have as many open loops nested together as we want. However, in practice we need to limit the number of nested open loops if we want to solve the puzzle in our lifetime! The *Chinese Rings* puzzle below is a good illustration of why.

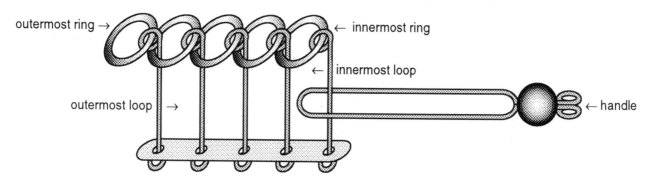

This puzzle got its name from all the rings that are used to nest the open loops. In the above example we have five rings that help to form four nested open loops. The handle on the right is a closed loop that is interlocked with the innermost nested loop. Most of the time, a *Chinese Rings* puzzle in its initial state has the handle locked inside the innermost loop only. The objective of the puzzle is to free the handle from the puzzle.

In the *Chinese Rings* puzzle, the handle has a slot large enough for the rings to move in and out of, and, at the same time, the end of the handle is narrow enough to slide in and out of the rings.

Let's number the rings and nested loops for easy reference. If we number the outermost ring as the first, then in the example below the innermost ring will be the fifth ring. The nested loops are numbered the same way, from outermost to innermost, using the numbers 1 to 4. In the figure below, the handle is locked in the second nested loop only.

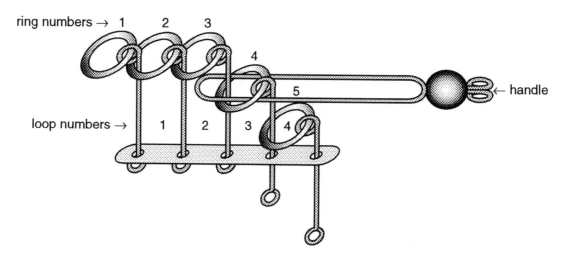

Solving the Chinese Rings Puzzles

It is best if you have a model of the *Chinese Rings* puzzle at hand when following the steps to solve the puzzle. In a *Chinese Rings* puzzle, a ring can have one of two positions in relation to the handle: either on the handle or off the handle. A ring is on the handle when the wire stem connected to the ring passes through the slot of the handle and the ring is either around the handle or can be pushed around the handle. A ring is off the handle when its stem either does not pass through the slot of the handle or, even if it does, the ring cannot be put around the handle. In the example given earlier, the third and fourth rings are on the handle, while the first, second, and fifth rings are off the handle. We can use the on and off positions to describe a sequence of moves that enables us to put a particular ring on the handle or take it off the handle. A three-ring *Chinese Rings* puzzle is the simplest, so we'll solve the three-ring model to start with. In addition, we'll simplify the graphic representation of the puzzle, as shown below.

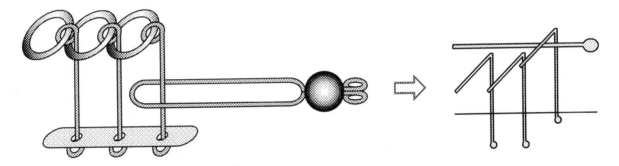

When making a move in solving the *Chinese Rings* puzzle, we either put a ring on the handle or take a ring off the handle. Let's take a look at some of these move sequences. To put the first ring on the handle, we can simply slide it up through the slot of the handle; to take it off the handle, we can do the reverse, sliding it back down through the slot of the handle. To put only the second ring on the handle, we first have to put the first ring on, then put the second ring on, and finally take the first ring off. To free the handle from the second ring requires the reverse sequence of moves: first put the first ring on, then take the second ring off, and finally take the first ring off. It seems that in order to put the second ring on or take the second ring off the handle, the first ring must be on the handle. Is it true that to put on or take off any ring other than the first one, the ring before the selected ring has to be on the handle?

Let's look at the three-ring example and try to free the handle from the third ring.

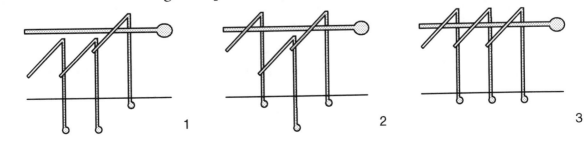

Exploring Math Through Puzzles

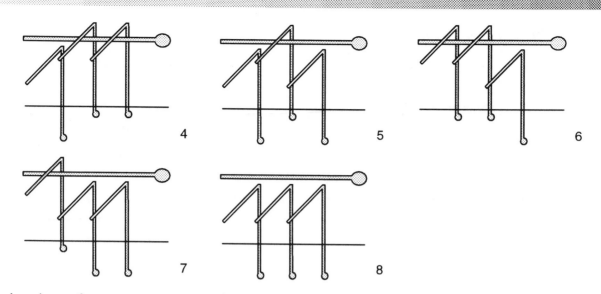

In the above figures, a ring is on the handle if it is shown with the handle passing through it. Figure 1 shows the initial state of the puzzle, with the third ring on the handle. Figures 2 through 8 show a step-by-step sequence of moves that will free the handle from the third ring. To determine a particular move, just compare the corresponding figure with the following figure.

Now let's make a generalization about how a ring can be moved on or off the handle. If it is the first ring, then it can be moved on or off directly. To move any other ring on or off the handle, first the ring before it has to be moved on, then the selected ring can be moved on or off, and finally the ring before it can be moved off again.

To summarize, we use functions *PutOn(n)* and *TakeOff(n)* to produce the steps of moving the *n*th ring on and off the handle. *PutOn(n)* initially has all the rings up to and including the *n*th ring off the handle, and it will put the *n*th ring on the handle and all the rings before the *n*th ring will be off the handle. *TakeOff(n)* initially has the *n*th ring on the handle and all rings before the *n*th ring are off the handle, and it will take the *n*th ring off the handle and all rings before the *n*th ring will also be off the handle. The on's and off's are direct moves.

$$
\text{PutOn(n)} = \begin{cases} \text{on n} & \text{if n = 1} \\ \text{PutOn(n--1), on n, TakeOff(n--1)} & \text{if n > 1} \end{cases}
$$

$$
\text{TakeOff(n)} = \begin{cases} \text{off n} & \text{if n = 1} \\ \text{PutOn(n--1), off n, TakeOff(n--1)} & \text{if n > 1} \end{cases}
$$

Do the functions work? I think so, but let's verify them by substituting some numbers in them and seeing what steps we get. We know how to take the second ring off the handle already, so let's see what we get from TakeOff(2).

TakeOff(2) = PutOn(1), off 2, TakeOff(1)
        = on 1, off 2, off 1

Now let's free the handle from the third ring.

TakeOff(3) = PutOn(2), off 3, TakeOff(2)
        = PutOn(1), on 2, TakeOff(1), off 3, PutOn(1), off 2, TakeOff(1)
        = on 1, on 2, off 1, off 3, on 1, off 2, off 1

It works! We get exactly the same steps in words as were pictured in figures 1 through 8 earlier.

Naturally, if you want to take off the handle, you first have to put it onto the puzzle. To put the third ring on the handle, we need to use PutOn(3). The written steps produced by PutOn(3) should match the steps shown in figures 1 through 8 (for moving the third ring off the handle) in reverse order.

PutOn(3)   = PutOn(2), on 3, TakeOff(2)
        = PutOn(1), on 2, TakeOff(1), on 3, PutOn(1), off 2, TakeOff(1)
        = on 1, on 2, off 1, on 3, on 1, off 2, off 1.

Using the *PutOn* and *TakeOff* functions, we should be able to generate a sequence of moves to solve a *Chinese Rings* puzzle having any number of rings. However, as we warned you earlier, you probably do not want to nest too many open loops in a *Chinese Rings* puzzle, or you could be spending the rest of your life solving the puzzle!

How many moves are needed to move the *n*th ring on or off the handle? We know by counting the *on*'s and *off*'s from our previous calculations that when $n = 2$, the number of moves is 3, and when $n = 3$, the number of moves is 7. What is the relationship between the number of moves and *n*? Since we know that each *on* or *off* counts as one move, we then can turn the *PutOn* and *TakeOff* functions into the counting functions *PutOnMoves* and *TakeOffMoves* as follows:

$$PutOnMoves(n) = \begin{cases} 1 & \text{if } n = 1 \\ PutOnMoves(n-1) + 1 + TakeOffMoves(n-1) & \text{if } n > 1 \end{cases}$$

$$TakeOffMoves(n) = \begin{cases} 1 & \text{if } n = 1 \\ PutOnMoves(n-1) + 1 + TakeOffMoves(n-1) & \text{if } n > 1 \end{cases}$$

Both counting functions work the same way, so we can simplify our counting by using just one function.

$$Moves(n) = \begin{cases} 1 & \text{if } n = 1 \\ Moves(n-1) + 1 + Moves(n-1) = 2 \times Moves(n-1) + 1 & \text{if } n > 1 \end{cases}$$

Let's try $n = 3$ to see if we get the number 7:

$$
\begin{aligned}
\text{Moves}(3) &= 2 \times \text{Moves}(2) + 1 \\
&= 2 \times (2 \times \text{Moves}(1) + 1) + 1 \\
&= 2 \times (2 \times 1 + 1) + 1 \\
&= 2 \times (2 + 1) + 1 \\
&= 4 + 2 + 1 \\
&= 7
\end{aligned}
$$

Indeed, we need seven moves to solve a *Chinese Rings* puzzle with three rings! Given that Moves(1) = 1, Moves(2) = 1 + 2 (see above), and Moves(3) = 1 + 2 + 4, can you guess what Moves(4) is? It is 1 + 2 + 4 + 8 = 15. Since we know that $2^0 = 1$, $2^1 = 2$, $2^2 = 4$, and $2^3 = 8$, we can deduce: $\text{Moves}(n) = 2^0 + 2^1 + 2^2 + 2^3 + \ldots + 2^{(n-1)} = 2^n - 1$.

With the growth of n, *Moves(n)* grows exponentially larger. If we can make one move every second, assuming that we do not make any wrong moves, how long does it take to solve a *Chinese Rings* puzzle with five rings, as in our example? How about nine rings? That's the number of rings in commercially available *Chinese Rings* puzzles. How many rings could we handle in our lifetime if we were to live 100 years and spend two thirds of our life moving the rings at the rate of one move per second?

Following is a table showing the length of time in years, days, hours, minutes, and seconds that it would take to solve a *Chinese Rings* puzzle with up to 32 rings. (See Activity 12—Math with the *Chinese Rings*, page 111.)

Number of rings	years	days	hours	minutes	seconds
1					1
2					3
3					7
4					15
9				8	31
10				17	3
15			9	6	7
20		12	3	16	15
25	1	23	8	40	31
30	34	17	13	37	3
31	68	35	3	14	7
32	136	70	6	28	15

I think I could be happy with as many as nine rings. How about you? By the way, have you heard of the *Tower of Hanoi* puzzle? There is much similarity between these two puzzles in terms of strategy and the counting of moves.

Knot Equivalence Puzzles

In mathematical knot theory, a **knot** is a curve without any thickness whose ends are joined together. In the physical world a knot can be made out of string, wire, or any other bendable linear material. When a knot is tied to a rigid object, such as a post or a ring, it is said to be **hitched** to that object. A picture of a knot is called a **projection** of the knot. The points where a knot projection crosses itself are called the **crossings** of the projection. The knot projection on the left below has no crossings. Each of the other two projections has three crossings.

Every knot has many different projections. The two figures on the right above are projections of the same knot, the **trefoil knot**. Can you visualize how one projection can be transformed into the other? If not, experiment with a piece of string.

Two knot projections are **equivalent** if they are projections of the same knot. A puzzle based on knot equivalence can be solved only by transforming the knot projection in the initial state of the puzzle to an **equivalent projection**. A knot equivalence puzzle has to have two essential components: a string (or something that functions as a string) and a rigid object with a hole, such as a ring. First the string is hitched to the hole, and then its ends are tied together or attached to other components of the puzzle to form a closed loop. The string must be hitched in such a way that its crossing positions in relation to the object to which it is hitched are in "over-over" and "under-under" pairs.

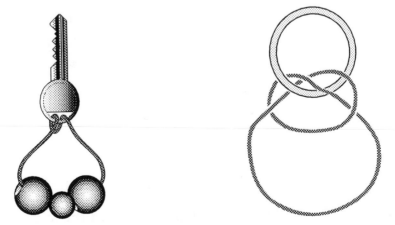

For example, in the *Key Tag* puzzle on the left, if we follow the string on the right-hand side toward the key, the crossings are "over-under-under-over." Since the string is tied in a loop, the two "overs" can be considered next to each other. The knot on the right does not satisfy the above condition because its crossings are "over-under-over-under."

Exploring Math Through Puzzles 25

Oftentimes in a knot equivalence puzzle, one or more objects are threaded on the string and are too large to pass through the hole in the hitched object. In *Key Tag*, a small bead and two large beads are threaded on a string that is hitched onto a key. In the puzzle's initial state, the small bead and the key separate the two large beads. To solve the puzzle you have to move the two large beads next to each other.

Let's take a close look at the *Key Tag* puzzle to see how the knot equivalence principle works. It appears that the only possible way to get the two large beads next to each other is by moving one of them back and forth through the key's hole to reach the other side of the small bead. But the key's hole is far too small for a large bead to pass through. Is it possible for one large bead to follow the string to the other large bead without passing through the key's hole? We'll find out soon.

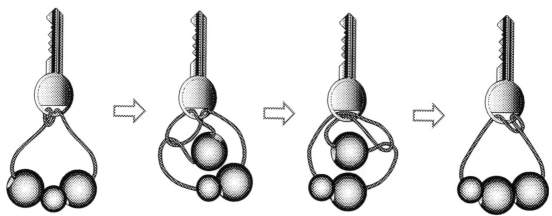

Let's try to move the large bead on the left to the other side by following the string. The string has one crossing point, and the bead must pass this crossing point twice in its journey to the other side. First move the bead toward the key and under the crossing point. It's easy if you first pull the string to make the loop big enough for the bead to pass. Next, it looks as though the bead has to pass through the key's hole before it can make the second crossing. Since passing through the key's hole is out of the question, we pull the entire crossing through the hole to the front side of the key. Now the bead can easily make the second crossing. After that, the two large beads are next to each other!

Now compare the knots of the initial and final states of the puzzle. The two knots look different, but they are the same knot—just different projections. *Key Tag* is a rather easy puzzle to solve, however the knot equivalence principle is just as useful in solving more difficult puzzles. When solving knot equivalence puzzles, just remember to follow the path of the string and to transform the initial projection of the knot if necessary.

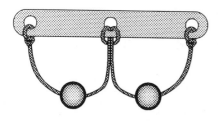

The *African Bead Puzzle* on the left is another knot equivalence puzzle. It has a square knot hitched on the center hole in the puzzleboard. Each end of the string is threaded through a bead and then attached to an end hole. The objective? Join the beads.

Untangling Puzzles

In mathematical knot theory, a knot is a closed loop with some crossings, and there is no way you can untie a knot without cutting the loop open. The kind of knot we use in daily life is a nonmathematical knot, because it is just a tangled up string with two loose ends. A nonmathematical knot can be untied by simply untangling the string. We all know how to tie and untie shoelaces, and if we are patient we can untie any other tangled up string, too. A puzzle based on untying a nonmathematical knot is called an **untangling** puzzle.

An untangling puzzle consists of a length of string hitched onto a hole in a rigid object in such a way that the string makes crossings through itself. As in a knot equivalence puzzle, the string must be hitched so that its crossing positions in relation to the object to which it is hitched are in "over-over" and "under-under" pairs. Although the objectives of two untangling puzzles may seem very different from each other, more often than not we'll solve both by untying the knots in them.

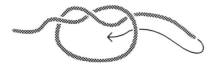

How do we untie a knot? We know that a knot is formed by having crossings in a string, so to untie a knot we have to undo the crossings. A crossing can be undone by moving one end of the string backwards through the string loop at the nearest crossing point, as shown above. To untie a knot, we take one loose end of the string and backtrack along the string until all the crossings are undone.

On the left is a simple untangling puzzle, *Keyed Off.* In this puzzle the string is tied around the hole of a key and both ends of the string are threaded through a large bead that slides freely between the knot and the ends of the string. Each end of the string has a small bead attached to it to stop the large bead from sliding off the ends. As its name suggests, the objective of this puzzle is to remove the key from the string. Since the string is hitched onto the key with a knot, we'll have to untie the knot in order to remove the key from the string. How do we untie the knot? Well, we see that there is one crossing in the knot, so all we have to do to untie the knot is undo this crossing.

One way to undo the crossing is to take the end of string on the left (with the small, dark-colored bead) and pass it back through the string loop at the crossing point. But the large bead is in the way, and the end of the string cannot pass through the hole in the large bead because of the small bead fastened on the end.

Is there another way to undo the crossing that doesn't require moving the end of the string through the large bead? Yes, we can move the crossing to the other side of the

Exploring Math Through Puzzles

large bead. Just pull the string loop as far as possible and thread it through the large bead. Once the loop has been pulled through the large bead, we can push the small bead through it to undo the crossing. Be careful not to twist the loop, or you'll add more crossings to the knot. When the crossing has been undone, the key, the large bead, and the beaded string all come apart.

The *Hitched Knot* puzzle below is a little harder, but the principle works just the same. In this puzzle, one end of the string is attached to an end hole of a puzzleboard and the other end of the string is threaded through a center hole in the puzzleboard and then attached to a bead. The bead is too large to pass through the holes in the puzzleboard. The center part of the string is hitched to the other end hole of the puzzleboard, and your objective is to unhitch that knot.

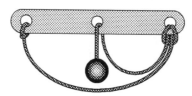

There are two crossings in the string. We have to undo both of them in order to untie the knot. Since the bead attached to the loose end of the string cannot pass through the holes in the puzzleboard, we have to pull the string loop and thread it through the back side of the center hole. Then we can push the bead through it to undo the first crossing, as shown in the left figure below.

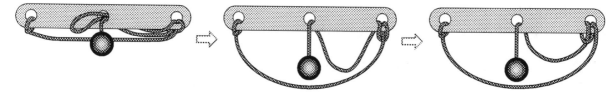

Now only one crossing is left, but the loop is around the end of the string attached to the puzzleboard (center figure), making it impossible to undo the crossing from that end. Can we undo the crossing from the loose end of the string? To do that, we'll have to move the crossing to the other side of the hole so that the loop will be around the loose end of the string. Remember knot equivalence? We can transform the knot projection in the center figure to the one on the right. After the crossing has been moved through the hole in the puzzleboard, the rest is easy.

Some puzzles incorporate several principles—open loop, knot equivalence, and untangling, for example—in their solutions. *The Arch* is one such puzzle. Initially, there is no knot in *The Arch*. But to solve the puzzle, you'll first have to make a knot, then transform the knot to another projection, and, finally, untie the knot. If you enjoy challenges, *The Arch* will not disappoint you.

Loop Extension Puzzles

A **loop extension** puzzle always has a string loop that seems to be too short to allow the puzzle to be solved. If only the string were a little longer! But if you understand the loop extension principle, you'll be able to find a way to extend the string loop and solve the puzzle.

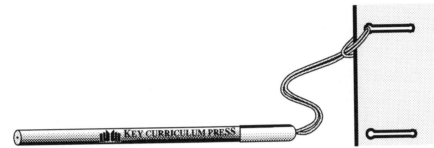

The *Magic Pencil* is a very well known loop extension puzzle. It consists of a regular pencil with a string loop attached to one end, and the string loop is shorter than the length of pencil. The figure above shows the puzzle in its initial state with the string loop hitched around a buttonhole. To solve the puzzle, we have to remove the pencil from the buttonhole.

In order to take the pencil off without cutting the string or shortening the pencil, we'll have to unhitch the knot. To unhitch the knot we'll have to undo its crossings by backtracking the ends of the string that are attached to the pencil. Since the ends of the string are attached to one end of the pencil, and the pencil is a rigid object, it appears that the string loop would have to be longer than the pencil to enable the pencil to pass through it. But it is not. This is what frustrates most people attempting to remove the pencil.

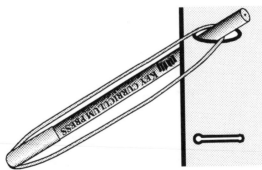

The loop extension principle tells us to look for an extension to the string loop in some other part of the puzzle. The other part of the *Magic Pencil* puzzle consists of the buttonhole and the rest of the shirt. Topologically, the buttonhole and the shirt can be represented as a small string loop on the end of a string. Let's use this simplified model to solve the puzzle.

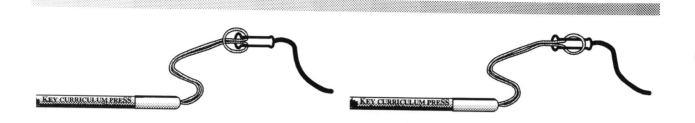

As shown in the first figure above, we now have a buttonhole loop with a length of string (instead of a shirt) attached to it. The string loop on the pencil and the buttonhole loop are hitched together into a square knot. The second figure above shows a different projection of this square knot. To unhitch a square knot formed out of two loops, we can backtrack one loop through the hole of the other loop. If we backtrack the string attached to the buttonhole loop, then we need to pass the entire shirt through the loop attached to the pencil. We can do this if the "victim" is willing to take off the shirt, but that could be embarrassing. Instead, let's see if we can find a way to take the pencil off the buttonhole by backtracking the pencil. That way, we can remove the pencil without making somebody take off the shirt.

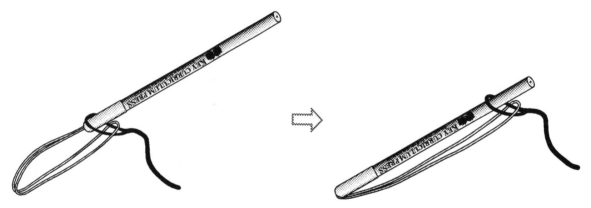

Let's backtrack the pencil by pushing its stringed end through the buttonhole loop (left figure) as far as possible. The pencil stops when the string loop has been fully extended (right figure). Unfortunately, the string loop on the pencil is not long enough to allow the pencil to slide all the way out of the buttonhole or to loop over the end of the pencil. How can we extend the string so that the pencil can continue backtracking out of the buttonhole loop? We can do it by using the string attached to the buttonhole loop to extend the string loop (figure below). Indeed, we can now free the pencil!

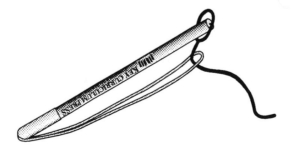

To see how this works on a real shirt, just imagine that the string and buttonhole loop in the figures have been replaced with a real shirt. We can extend the string loop by pulling the shirt's buttonhole (and part of the shirt) through the string loop. If we pull the buttonhole far enough, we can slip it over the end of the pencil, and the pencil is free.

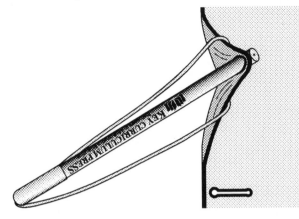

Magic Pencil is a classic puzzle due to its ingenuity and simplicity of design. Most people never think of the shirt as being part of the puzzle. That's why *Magic Pencil* can be so baffling. Many people will carefully observe how you attach the pencil to the buttonhole, but later they will insist that the string is simply too short to allow the pencil to be taken off!

The other loop extension puzzle included in this book is *Yoked Bead*, in which strings and small beads are used to lock a large bead onto a puzzleboard yoke. The objective is to free the large bead from the rest of the puzzle.

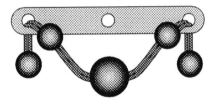

Just looking at the puzzle, as shown in the above figure, gives us no clue as to its solution. But what if we tell you that hidden inside the hole of the large bead is a square knot formed by two string loops? Mind you, neither string loop is long enough to reach the opposite end of the puzzleboard. But what if you could extend one of the loops?

Folding-and-Twisting Puzzles

Finally, we have a class of puzzles that can be solved with the help of some strategic folding and twisting. A **folding-and-twisting** puzzle has a large ring locked around it. The ring seems to be hopelessly trapped on the puzzle, because the structure on each side of the ring's opening is too large for the ring to pass over. *Shackled Ring*, shown below, is an example of a folding-and-twisting puzzle.

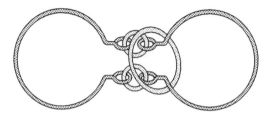

In *Shackled Ring*, a large ring is locked around the center of the puzzle where two shackles are joined together. Since both shackles are too large for the ring to pass over, the obvious exits for the ring are impossible. So we have to find another way to free the ring. Imagine that we could fold the two shackles together into two arches linked at the ends and have the ring hanging in the middle, as shown below. Then the ring could slide off the shackles on either end of the arches.

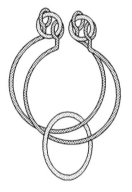

But how can we get from the initial state to the above state? Since the joined shackles form a loop structure, we can use a large string loop instead of the shackles to investigate how the ring and shackles work together.

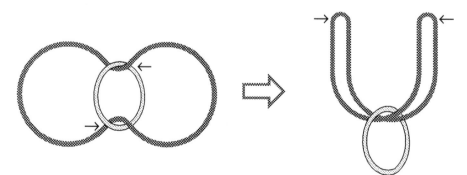

For the initial state, place the ring around the loop on a table, as shown above on the left. Next, pick up the string loop by two points close to, but on opposite sides of, the ring. When you pick up the string, observe how the ring drops down on the string loop. The ring makes a 90° twist or rotation as it changes from the initial state to the state in which it is ready to slide out of the string loop. What happens to the string loop? It actually folds into two half loops just like the shackles in the puzzle.

Now apply your understanding of the relationship between the string loop and the ring to the shackles and the ring, and the solution can be easily obtained.

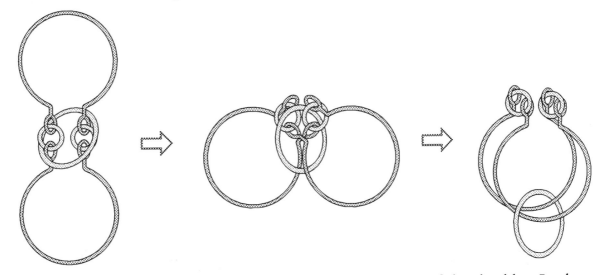

First position the ring so that it is diagonally across the center of the shackles. In the above left figure, the ring crosses from lower left to upper right. Next, slowly fold the shackles together, allowing the ring to slide down the openings of the arches, as shown in the center figure. Let the ring continue to drop until it is in the center of the two arches, as shown on the right. Finally, slide the ring out of the shackles on either end of the joined arches. If you want to put the ring on the shackles, just follow the figures in reverse order.

Shown above is *Lyon's Loops*, another puzzle based on folding-and-twisting. The large ring is locked in the puzzle by the two large loop structures and the triangle, which are too large for the ring to pass over. Can you free the ring from the puzzle? You'll have some folding to do.

Exploring Math Through Puzzles

Unclassified Puzzles

Some puzzles in this book have not yet been classified topologically. It is beyond the scope of this book to discuss in detail how or why these puzzles work. However, we'll point out a few issues involved in the solution of two of these puzzles, *Snail* and *No Way Out*. These two puzzles are noteworthy because of their intriguing designs and methods of solution. Interested readers are encouraged to write to us with your insights and explanations of the puzzles' underlying principles. Perhaps we'll be able to include your contribution in the next edition of this book.

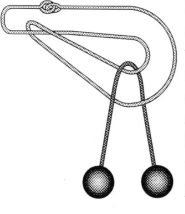

In *Snail*, there is a wire frame and a string with beads attached at the end. The wire frame can be formed by twisting a closed wire loop 360° into two connected loops and then folding them together to form a small interior loop and a large exterior loop. (Try doing this with a string loop.) A beaded string is locked in the puzzle through the small loop. The beads are too large to pass through the small loop or through the opening between the small and large loops. To solve the puzzle, you have to remove the beaded string from the *Snail*.

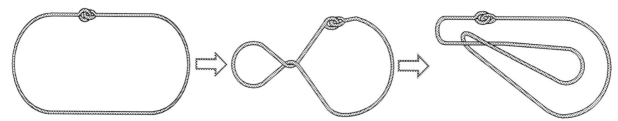

To understand how the string is trapped in the wire frame, we need to begin with the puzzle in its final (separated) state and work backwards. The figures below show the puzzle in its separated state (left), intermediate state (center), and initial state (right).

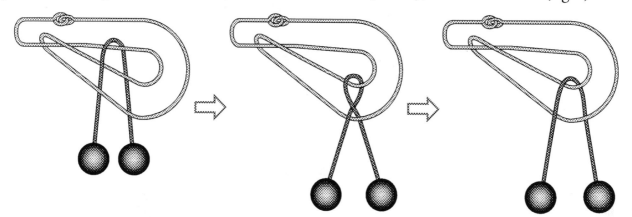

There are two crossings in the wire frame—the front one forms the small loop and the back one forms the large loop. First drape the beaded string over the small loop from the back side of the puzzle (left), and then slide it over the front crossing. Keep sliding it until it falls onto the back crossing. At this point the string is hanging from the wire shared by both crossings. Next, slide the string along the wire until it reaches the lowest point of the small loop (center). Now we have a string that is hanging from the center of the puzzle and that has a crossing between the small and large loops. Our knowledge of untangling puzzles helps us get rid of that crossing, and the puzzle is then in its initial state (right). Given the above, you should have no problem reversing the steps and removing the beaded string from the *Snail*.

What's interesting about the *Snail* is how the string is crossed with respect to the crossing of the small loop. Rotating the center figure 90° we can see that the small loop is crossed right-over-left from the top, while the string loop is crossed left-over-right. The crossings are the reverse of each other. Would we be able to remove the string if both crossings had the same orientation? How would you cross the string before removing it from the puzzle if the wire frame of the *Snail* was the mirror image of the above frame?

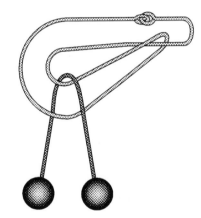

How would you solve the puzzle if a small ring was put around both ends of the string just above the beads?

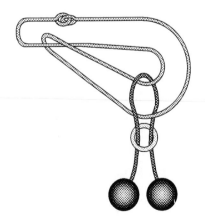

Exploring Math Through Puzzles 35

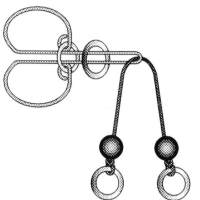

No Way Out has a ring locked between the puzzle's wire frame and a string structure that is threaded through a slot on the wire frame. In the string structure, a bead is threaded on each side of the wire slot and held by a ring tied to the string's end. The slot in the wire frame is large enough for the rings to pass through, but not the beads. As a result, the rings on the ends of the string stop the beads from coming off the string, and the beads stop the string from coming out of the slot. The ring locked in the center of the puzzle can pass over the beads, but not the other two rings. How do you free the locked ring?

We'd like to remove the string structure from the wire frame, but that is out of the question. So we have to remove the ring while the string structure is on the wire frame. Since the other side of the frame is too large to pass through the ring, the only exit is the end of the slot. But the string structure is in the way. Therefore, we have to figure out a way to manipulate the string structure to free the ring.

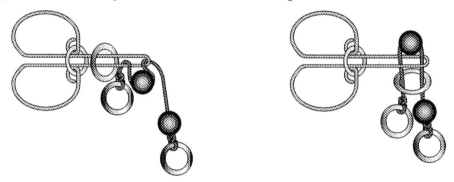

Let's first move one of the rings attached to the string through the slot (left figure). Next we slide the center ring all the way off the end of the slot. Then we pass the ring over the bead that is looped on one side of the slot. Now the ring is off the slot, but it is still around the string (right figure). To free the ring from the string, we can now move the ring through the slot to pass over that bead.

The key to this puzzle lies in the string structure. When the string is threaded back and forth through the slot and is held by a bead (right figure), it offers an opening to the ring hanging around it. At this point the puzzle can be compared to an open loop if we imagine the ends of the string attached to the lower handle of the wire frame.

Now we have some questions to test your understanding of the puzzle. Could the ring be freed in the same way if one end of the string was attached to one of the handles on the wire frame instead of a ring? How could you free the ring if the string was looped once around the slot in its initial state? How about twice? What complexity would looping the string bring to the puzzle?

Practical Tips

Your Puzzle Workshop

It is quite important that you have some work space to make the puzzles. It can be a real workshop, or it can be a makeshift workshop with only a table or desk and a chair. If yours is a makeshift workshop, it is important to have a storage place for your things so that you can set up and put away your workshop easily.

Creating Your Own Workbench

Before beginning to make the puzzles in this book, you should create a workspace where you can have your tools and materials organized and at hand. If a woodworking workbench is not available, any large flat surface, such as a desk or a kitchen table, will do. We suggest that you cover the work area of your "workbench" with a large paper grocery bag to protect the table or desk.

First, let's create the workbench. Cut off the bottom of the paper grocery bag and open up the bag into a rectangular sheet. Spread the sheet on your working surface with the blank side (the inside of the bag) facing up. Rotate the sheet so that the longer sides are horizontal from your perspective. Tape the sheet along the edge of the work surface where you'll be sitting.

Next, mark a ruler on the workbench to use when measuring string and wire. Use a ruler or straightedge (at least 12" long) to draw a straight line $1/2$" from the front edge of the paper. You can extend the line all the way to the side edges. Select a point near the left or the right end of the line, and mark it with a zero (0). (I like my zero point to be on the left end of the line, but you might find the right end more convenient.) Starting from the zero point, make a mark every 1" on the line until you have marked off 24". Now you have a workbench.

Tools and Materials in Your Workshop

In Appendix A, there is a list of tools and materials needed to make all 54 puzzles in this book. Among the tools you'll need are a ruler, scissors, and a lighter. The lighter is to be used to melt the ends of the nylon string so that they do not unravel. A box of tissues will come in handy for wiping off excess glue when gluing cubes.

When making the *Magic Pencil* puzzle, you will find it hard to thread the string loop through the hole in the metal pencil cap. We suggest that you make a threading aid to use whenever a puzzle requires you to thread string through a small hole. In the "Techniques and Skills—Working with String" section, we show you how to make your own threading aid.

Exploring Math Through Puzzles 37

Techniques and Skills

You don't have to be a skilled craftsperson to make the puzzles in this book. Some of the puzzles are very easy to make and require mostly common knowledge. However, we have included some puzzles that require a degree of skill and practice. In this section we introduce some methods and skills that will help you do your best work with the tools and materials you'll be using to create puzzles.

Working with Cubes

It is fairly easy to make the wood cube puzzles included in the book. Two of these puzzles only require you to apply colored stickers to the faces of a cube. For the others you must be able to join two cubes face to face using ticky-tac or wood glue. When making wood cube puzzles, you should constantly compare your work with the figures on the puzzle instruction pages. When making the polycube pieces for the cube construction puzzles, you can build the pieces using ticky-tac before permanently gluing them.

Using ticky-tac: Ticky-tac is used to stick wood cubes together temporarily. First take a small, pea-sized portion of ticky-tac and press it onto the face of a cube. Then take another cube and press it face to face with the first cube, squeezing the ticky-tac between the two cubes. Correct the alignment of the cubes by twisting and pressing them together, if necessary. Ticky-tac can easily be removed from the surface of the cubes and reused. To remove small, stubborn traces of ticky-tac from a cube, take a large portion of ticky-tac and repeatedly press it on the traces to be removed and pull it away quickly.

Using glue: Glue is used to permanently attach the wood cubes. It takes a few trials to figure out exactly how much glue to use to attach two cubes face to face. The face of a cube has either side grain or end grain. A cut parallel to the growth of a tree yields side-grained faces, and a cut across the growth of a tree yields end-grained faces. An end-grained face tends to soak up more glue than a side-grained face. Therefore, you need to apply a little more glue to an end-grained face. Use a tissue to wipe off any excess glue before it dries, and let your polycubes dry for at least 30 minutes before using them.

Finishing polycubes: If you like, you can help to preserve and beautify your polycube pieces by applying a mineral oil finish. Apply a thin layer of mineral oil with a tissue, then let the oil soak in. The wood will appear a little darker after application of the mineral oil.

Working with Wire

Of all the puzzles in this book, the wire puzzles are unquestionably the most challenging to make. I suggest that you use 14-gauge wire, which can be found in most hardware stores. The wire from coat-hangers is easily available, but it is harder to work with. On the puzzle instruction pages, all figures of wire puzzles (and puzzles with wire components), except *Chinese Rings*, have been drawn to scale. So when making each wire part of a puzzle, constantly compare it to the figure on the instruction page. Any measurement of the diameter of a wire loop or eye refers to its outside diameter. A pair of needle-nose pliers is all you need to cut and bend the wire.

For most of the wire parts, each end is either bent into an end loop or an eye. Always try to form the end loops and eyes before bending the center of the wire, unless otherwise stated in the instructions. It is much easier to work on the ends of the wire when you have a lot of room. If the part has a symmetrical structure, like the clef puzzles, then start bending from the center of the wire and work toward both ends alternately to assure symmetry. Make the simpler puzzles before attempting to make puzzles with complicated wire parts. You will get more skillful at working with wire as you gain experience.

Measuring and cutting wire: First straighten out the wire from one end and measure it against your ruler. Then hold the wire near the cutoff point and cut it by squeezing it between the cutting edges of the pliers.

Bending an end loop: If possible, bend the end loops of a wire part first. Hold the pliers in one hand and the wire in the other. Start bending the wire at the tip, and only bend a little at a time as you move away from the tip. Stop when the desired size (about $5/8$" in outside diameter) is reached. Then center the loop by bending the wire at the point where the tip of the loop touches the beginning of the loop.

Bending an eye: Again, you want to do this before bending the rest of the wire. An eye is a very small loop (about $3/8$" in outside diameter) that is used to join the ends of the wire together or to lock a small ring inside. Bend an eye the same way you bend an end loop. If an eye is used to join the ends of a wire together, then it does not have to be nice and round.

Interlocking eyes: We interlock two eyes either to join the ends of one wire into a loop or to join two separate pieces of wire together. First, leave one of the eyes open and close the other one by squeezing it with your pliers. Next, stick the end of the open eye through the loop of the closed eye, and then close the open eye.

Bending a right angle: Many wire parts have rectangular shapes, so there are a lot of right angles to bend. First grip the wire in the center of the pliers, with the point where the right angle is to be formed at the inside edge of the pliers. Then use your free hand to hold the wire firmly while you twist the pliers until the desired angle is reached.

Finishing touch: After completing each wire part, carefully check it and use the pliers to smooth out any crooked sections.

Working with Puzzleboards and Beads

A puzzleboard is made out of a thick tongue depressor with three $1/4$"-diameter holes drilled in it. Sanding is the only preparation puzzleboards and beads require. The holes in puzzleboards need to be sanded so that they are smooth enough for strings to pass through without catching on small slivers of wood. Sometimes you also need to sand the holes in medium-sized and large beads. Do not sand the small beads, because they are used mostly for hiding knots inside their holes and a little roughness actually helps to secure the knots tightly.

To sand a hole in a bead or puzzleboard, roll up a small piece of sandpaper and move the rolled-up sandpaper back and forth through the hole. You can roll the sandpaper around a nail or thin dowel if you want more firmness. If you have access to a set of small (needlepoint) files, you can use a round-shaped file to get rid of most of the roughness before finishing up with sandpaper.

Working with String

Whenever we use a string to make a puzzle, we always end up tying some kind of knot. Some puzzles have string loops, so we must know how to tie some knots that join two ends of string together. We call these **joining knots**. Other puzzles require the ends of the string to be attached to puzzleboards or small beads, so we must also be able to tie knots that can be used to fasten string to other objects. Below, we show you how to make a few knots that we recommend for use in making puzzles. Which knot to use for which puzzle is up to you. In addition, we show you how to make a threading aid you can use when you need to thread a string through a small hole.

Sealing the ends of a string: I prefer using nylon string. However, it will unravel at the ends unless they are sealed. The ends of a nylon string can be sealed by melting them with a lighter or a candle. Just heat the string long enough to melt the ends; do not burn them or let them catch on fire. Do this with caution and make sure there is adult supervision when children are doing it.

Tying an overhand end knot: This is a knot we all learned early in our lives. In making these puzzles, we frequently tie this knot at the very end of a string to stop a small bead from coming off. If an overhand end knot is not large enough to hold a bead tightly, make the knot bigger by looping the ends twice.

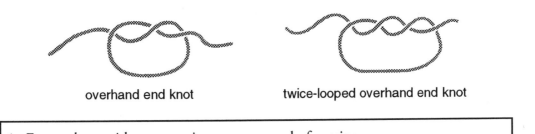

overhand end knot   twice-looped overhand end knot

> 1. Form a loop with one crossing near one end of a string.
> 2. Take the same end of the string and thread it through the loop.
> 3. Pull both ends of the string to make the knot tight.

Tying a sheet bend knot: This is my favorite joining knot. It is a secure knot and it ties relatively smaller than other types of joining knots.

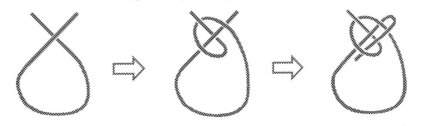

> 1. Cross the left end of the string over the right end. Hold the crossing point between two fingers of one hand.
> 2. Hold the right side of the loop between two fingers of your other hand and loop it behind what is now the left end of the string.
> 3. Fold what is now the right end of the string over the right side and under the left side of the new loop.
> 4. Finally, pull both ends of the string to make the knot tight.

Tying a square knot: This popular joining knot is essentially two overhand knots—one tied on top of the other.

> 1. First make an overhand knot.
> 2. Then tie another overhand knot on top of the first one. Make sure that the two overhand knots are symmetric to each other. Otherwise, the knot will not be secure enough.
> 3. Finally, pull the ends of the string to make the knot tight.

Making a string loop: Just tie the two ends of the string together with a joining knot.

Making a beaded string loop: Double up the string and thread the doubled-up end through a small bead. Tie a joining knot at the very end of the string, but don't make it

     Exploring Math Through Puzzles

too tight. Pull the bead to cover up the knot. If a joining knot is too big to go into the hole of the bead, tie the ends together with a tight overhand end knot instead.

Attaching a bead to the end of a string: First thread the string through the bead, and then tie an overhand end knot at the end of the string. Pull the bead over the knot to cover it up tightly. If the overhand knot is not big enough, retie it with two loops.

Attaching the end of a string to another object: In some puzzles, the ends of the strings are attached to other objects, such as holes in a puzzleboard or eyes in a wire part of the puzzle. When the string is attached, it must stay attached. First thread the end of the string through the hole in the object. Then tie the end to the other side of the string with a joining knot.

Making a threading aid: It helps a lot if you use a threading aid for threading a string through a small hole. You need to find a 4" length of plastic-coated twister wire (the kind that comes with electric cord) and an object with a hole in it (such as a bead, a ring, or a key) to use as the handle. Thread the twister through the hole in the handle so that one end sticks out of the hole about $2^{1}/_{2}$", and then twist both ends of the twister close to the handle to secure it there. Peel the plastic coating off the long end of the twister, and bend a $^{3}/_{8}$" hook at the end. You can use this threading aid to thread a string through the hole of a pencil cap or a small bead.

Threading a string loop through the hole in a pencil cap: You do need something to help a string loop pass through the small hole in a pencil cap, and the threading aid works well. Push the threading aid through the hole from outside of the pencil cap. Next, loop the string over the hook, and pull the threading aid together with the string back through the hole. Finally, take off the threading aid and pull the string loop until it is stopped by the knot.

Cutting Cardboard Tubes and Plastic Cups

Cutting out a cardboard tube: Take a cardboard tube from a pants hanger of the type that you get from a dry cleaner. Cut off a piece of the tube that is slightly longer than the desired length, and carefully trim the edges by cutting narrow coils until the tube is the desired length.

Making a plastic cup: You need to find a plastic bottle that is soft enough to cut with scissors and punch holes in with a hand-held punch. The best ones are squeezable lotion and shampoo bottles. Mark the cutting line with a pen. Use the tip of a scissors blade to punch a hole in the bottle $^{1}/_{2}$" above the cutting line, and then cut the cup out of the bottle a little above the line. Carefully trim the edge of your cup to the cutting line.

Safety

We want you to have a pleasant experience when making the puzzles, and, most of all, we want you to be safe when using the tools and materials. Always use common sense and follow instructions when handling tools and materials that could potentially hurt you. Keep tools, glue, and the lighter away from small children. If you are using a tool or material for the first time or are not sure how to handle it, consult the instructions that came with it or ask someone for assistance.

Working with Tools

Use your tools; do not play with them! Most of the tools required for making the puzzles are common tools, and perhaps you have used some of them before. Some tools can cause personal and property damage if they are not handled properly. Use them only for their intended use, and put them away when they are not in use. We recommend that you store the tools in a box or cabinet.

Handling Fire

When a lighter or a candle is to be used to seal the ends of nylon strings, make sure that an adult is present to supervise. An adult should do this task for young children and for any others who may not be able to handle a lighter properly. Put the lighter away when it is not in use. If a candle is used to seal the ends of string, set the candle securely and away from other materials. Put out the candle when not using it.

Toxic Material

The fumes from melting nylon string may be toxic, so it is best to work outside or near an open window or door. The wood glue, although nontoxic, should never be taken internally, and any excess should be washed from your hands after finishing a gluing job.

Avoid Being Hurt

If you are not careful, even paper can cut you. Common things can hurt you if they are not handled correctly. The burrs formed when wire is cut are sharp, so be very careful when you handle wire.

Diabolical Cube

Don't be fooled by the name of this puzzle! It is, in fact, one of the simplest $3 \times 3 \times 3$ cube puzzles. It was named "diabolical" because there are 13 different ways to put the six pieces together to form a $3 \times 3 \times 3$ cube. This puzzle was described by Professor Hoffmann (Angelo John Lewis) in *Puzzles Old and New*, published in London in 1893.

The six puzzle pieces contain 2, 3, 4, 5, 6, and 7 cubes, respectively, and all the pieces are flat. All the pieces also have reflexive symmetry; that is, you can divide the piece into two parts along an imaginary plane (either vertical, horizontal, or diagonal) so that the two parts are mirror images of each other. See how many planes of symmetry you can find for each piece.

Materials Required

- 27 2-cm wooden cubes
- wood glue
- sandpaper
- mineral oil (optional)

Making the Puzzle

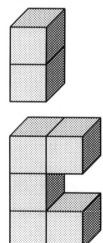

1. Arrange the cubes into sets of 2, 3, 4, 5, 6, and 7 cubes.
2. Glue each set of cubes together to form one of the puzzle pieces. Refer to the figures below as you glue the cubes together. Let the glue dry for half an hour.

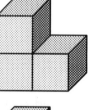
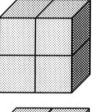

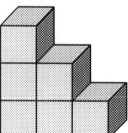
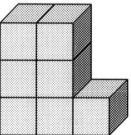

3. Sand the pieces smooth, if necessary.
4. (Optional) Apply a thin layer of mineral oil to each piece.

Solving the Puzzle

Put the six pieces together to form a $3 \times 3 \times 3$ cube.

Soma Cube

Piet Hein is the inventor of the *Soma Cube*. Legend has it that this Danish poet and puzzle inventor devised the *Soma Cube* while he was listening to a lecture on quantum physics in 1936.

The seven pieces in the puzzle represent all the ways that three or four cubes can be arranged other than in a rectangular shape. There are 240 different ways of putting the seven pieces together to form a 3 × 3 × 3 cube!

Can you identify the five pieces that have reflexive symmetry?

Materials Required

- 27 2-cm wooden cubes
- wood glue
- sandpaper
- mineral oil (optional)

Making the Puzzle

1. Arrange the cubes into sets of four cubes. You'll get six sets of four cubes and one set of three cubes left over.

2. Glue each set of cubes together to form one of the puzzle pieces shown below. Let the glue dry for half an hour.

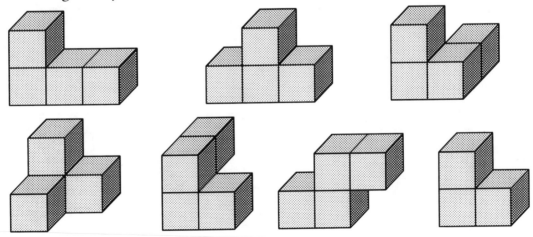

3. Sand the pieces smooth, if necessary.
4. (Optional) Apply a thin layer of mineral oil to each piece.

Solving the Puzzle

Put the seven pieces together to form a 3 × 3 × 3 cube.

Variations

Use all the pieces to construct some interesting shapes and objects.

Exploring Math Through Puzzles

Stewart T. Coffin, a well-known puzzle inventor from Massachusetts, once investigated six-piece versions of the $3 \times 3 \times 3$ cube. However, he found that there were several thousand possible ways to make three four-cube pieces and three five-cube pieces. Some of the configurations had many solutions and some had none. Finally Mr. Coffin found this configuration that has exactly one solution, and he produced it in 1980 as the *Half-Hour Cube*.

Can you identify the three pieces that have reflexive symmetry? Can you locate all their planes of symmetry?

Materials Required

- 27 2-cm wooden cubes
- wood glue
- sandpaper
- mineral oil (optional)

Making the Puzzle

1. Arrange the cubes into three sets of four cubes and three sets of five cubes.
2. Refer to the figures below as you glue each set of cubes together. Let the glue dry for half an hour.

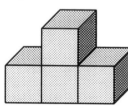 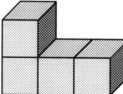 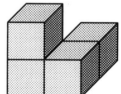

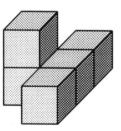 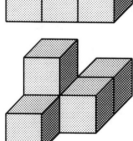 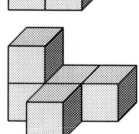

3. Sand the pieces smooth, if necessary.
4. (Optional) Apply a thin layer of mineral oil to each piece.

Solving the Puzzle

Put the six pieces together to form a $3 \times 3 \times 3$ cube.

This cube puzzle was invented by Nob Yoshigahara, a Japanese puzzle inventor and collector. Mr. Yoshigahara has also written many books and articles on puzzles. This puzzle uses five nonflat five-cube pieces and one two-cube piece.

There is only one way to put the six pieces together to form a $3 \times 3 \times 3$ cube, and it is not easy to find.

Materials Required

- 27 2-cm wooden cubes
- wood glue
- sandpaper
- mineral oil (optional)

Making the Puzzle

1. Arrange the cubes into sets of five cubes. You'll get five sets and two leftover cubes.
2. Refer to the figures below as you glue the cubes together. Let the glue dry for half an hour.

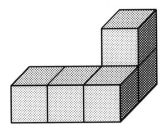 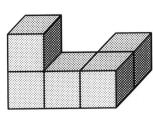 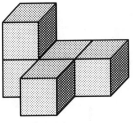

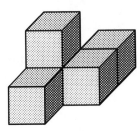 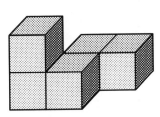 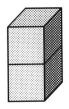

3. Sand the pieces smooth, if necessary.
4. (Optional) Apply a thin layer of mineral oil to each piece.

Solving the Puzzle

Put the six pieces together to form a $3 \times 3 \times 3$ cube.

This puzzle has been around since the turn of the century in many different forms. Basically, it is a set of four cubes with one of four different colors or patterns on each face. The first known version of this puzzle used the four playing card suits and was patented by Frederick A. Schossow in 1900. Others versions showed flags, coins, or product pictures for advertising.

This puzzle can be made from simple materials, such as paper or cardboard, or from fancy hardwood or marble. In 1967, Franz O. Armbruster, a California computer programmer, produced a plastic version of this puzzle and called it *Instant Insanity*. It caught the attention of the public and was a big success.

Instant Insanity is an **object orientation** puzzle. In this type of puzzle you have a set of objects that are identical in shape, but different in surface design (color, texture, or graphics). To solve the puzzle you have to arrange and orient the objects so that they satisfy some defined objective.

Materials Required

- 4 1" wooden cubes
- ³/₄"-diameter round colored stickers (6 <u>B</u>lue, 5 <u>G</u>reen, 6 <u>R</u>ed, and 7 <u>Y</u>ellow)

Making the Puzzle

Shown below are color layout plans of the four cubes. Apply colored stickers to the faces of the four cubes, as shown. Put the stickers on carefully, and check to make sure that each cube matches its layout.

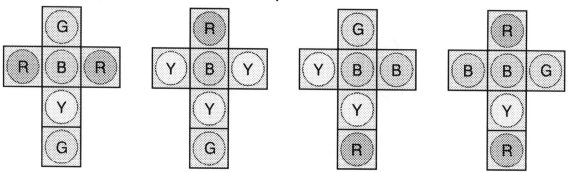

Solving the Puzzle

Arrange the cubes in a row so that all four colors appear on each of the row's four sides.

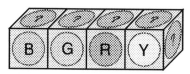

Bewitching Cubes

Here is another object orientation puzzle. The objects in this puzzle are six cubes. For each cube in this set, a different color appears on each of its six faces. The objective is to arrange the cubes in a row so that all six colors appear on each of the row's four sides. A version of this six-cube puzzle was patented in Great Britain by G. Moffat in 1900. It used the six initials of the general officers of the South African Field Forces on the sides.

Materials Required

- 6 1" wooden cubes
- 3/4"-diameter round colored stickers
  (6 each of Blue, Green, Red, Yellow, Orange, and Light Blue)

Making the Puzzle

 Apply colored stickers to the faces of the six cubes, as shown below. Each face of a cube should have a different color from the other five faces. Put the stickers on carefully, and check to make sure that each cube matches its layout.

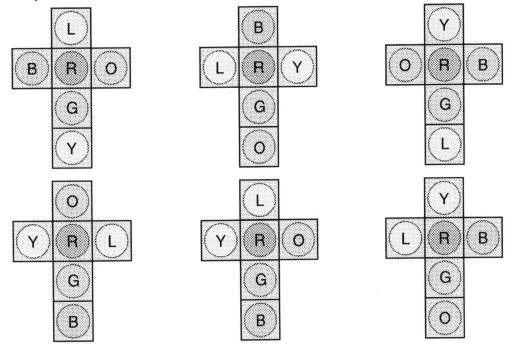

Solving the Puzzle

 Arrange the cubes in a row so that all six colors appear on each of the row's four sides, as shown below.

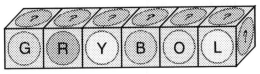

Exploring Math Through Puzzles

This puzzle was invented by the famous puzzle-maker Sam Loyd as an advertising gimmick for the New York Life Insurance Company. Have you ever heard the expression "to buttonhole somebody"? Well, you have now; and you definitely will have a better understanding of it after you've tried this puzzle. The pencil is attached to the buttonhole of a "victim," who is then challenged to take it off. The puzzle's simple design fools people into thinking it is easy and trivial—until they try to remove the pencil!

Materials Required

- 1 unsharpened, eraserless, round pencil
- 1 metal pencil cap with a hole
- 14" of thin string
- wood glue
- ruler
- scissors

Making the Puzzle

1. Cut a 14" length of thin string and seal the ends.
2. Double up the string and tie the ends together with a knot.
3. Stick the looped string inside the cap, and thread it through the hole until it is stopped by the knot. If you have trouble threading the string through the hole of the cap, refer to "Techniques and Skills—Working with String" in the section headed "Practical Tips." You may have to make a threading aid.
4. Apply two drops of wood glue to the inside of the cap, and then push the pencil all the way into the cap. Let it dry for at least 15 minutes.

Solving the Puzzle

Your first challenge is to attach the pencil to a buttonhole as shown below. Your next challenge is to remove the pencil from the buttonhole. We suggest that you practice doing this on your own shirt or jacket before trying it on a "victim."

Keyed Off

This original puzzle was chosen for its simplicity of design and availability of material. It is not a hard puzzle either. Here is proof. One day I handed this puzzle to my friend Don and asked him to solve it. After a very short time, with a grin on his face, Don displayed the key in one hand and the rest of the puzzle in the other. And guess what? Not only did he solve the puzzle in less than 15 minutes, but he also gave it a name: Keyed Off.

Materials Required

- 1 key (surely you can find an old key somewhere!)
- 2 small beads (preferably not the same color)
- 1 medium-sized bead
- 10" of thick string
- ruler
- scissors
- sandpaper

Making the Puzzle

1. Find a useless key that has a hole large enough for a doubled-up string to pass through freely.
2. Cut a 10" piece of thick string and seal the ends.
3. Loop the string in the key's hole, as shown above.
4. Roll up a very small piece of sandpaper and sand inside the hole of the medium-sized bead until it is smooth. Then thread both ends of the string through the bead.
5. Thread a small bead onto each end of the string. Then tie a knot at each end of the string, and pull the bead over the knot to hide it securely inside the hole.

Solving the Puzzle

As the puzzle's name suggests, you are supposed to take the key off the string. But don't get teed off if you can't get the key off right away. After you've taken it off, put it back on again.

This puzzle looks a lot like *Keyed Off*, since both have beads on a string attached to a key. However, there is a big difference! Even if you can solve *Keyed Off*, you might have a problem solving this puzzle. Don't try to take the key off the string (you can't without cutting the string)—just move the large beads so that they are next to each other on the string. Looks impossible? Try it to find out!

Materials Required

- 1 key (surely you can find an old key somewhere!)
- 10" of thick string
- 2 large beads
- 1 small bead
- ruler
- scissors
- sandpaper

Making the Puzzle

1. Find a useless key that has a hole large enough for a doubled-up string to pass through freely.
2. Cut a 10" piece of thick string and seal the ends.
3. Loop the string in the key's hole, as shown above.
4. Roll up a very small piece of sandpaper and sand inside the large beads until the holes are smooth. Then thread each end of the string through one bead.
5. Thread the small bead onto either end of the string, tie the ends of the string together with a knot, and pull the knot tightly inside the hole of the small bead.

Solving the Puzzle

Now the two large beads are separated by the small bead. Your job is to bring the two large beads together. Of course, the key and the small bead are in the way— but that is the challenge. Once you get the two large beads together, can you move them apart again?

This simple puzzle is easily made from things you can find in your house. The key to the puzzle lies in how the string is arranged inside the tube. It is a good puzzle for beginners to make and try to solve.

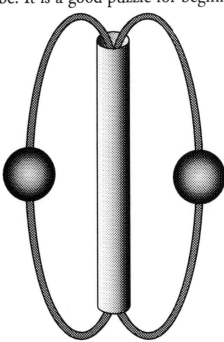

Materials Required

- 1 cardboard tube from a pants hanger
- 32" of thick string
- 2 large beads
- ruler
- scissors
- sandpaper

Making the Puzzle

1. Cut a 6" length of cardboard tube from a pants hanger.
2. Roll up a very small piece of sandpaper and sand the holes in two large beads to remove any rough edges.
3. Cut a 32" piece of thick string and seal the ends.
4. Double up the string and push the string's loop through the tube until a little loop sticks out of the opposite end of the tube.
5. Put a bead on each loose end of the string.
6. Push one loose end of the string through the little loop.
7. Tie the loose ends of the string together with a knot.
8. Pull the pair of strings out of one end of the tube until the interlocking loops and the knot are hidden inside the other end of the tube.

Solving the Puzzle

Join the two beads on the same section of the string. Of course, when the beads are together, then you can challenge your friends to separate them. Always be sure to hide the knot and the interlocking loops inside the tube before giving the puzzle to someone to solve.

Variation

The string originally is looped together inside the tube with just one crossing. How about forming a square knot (on the right) instead? This will definitely add more difficulty to the puzzle.

Exploring Math Through Puzzles

If *Trouble Tube* is too easy, you can *Double the Trouble* by adding on another tube. It is still easier than most of the puzzles in this collection. See for yourself by making and solving it.

Materials Required

- 1 cardboard tube from a pants hanger
- 44" of thick string
- 2 large beads
- ruler
- scissors
- sandpaper

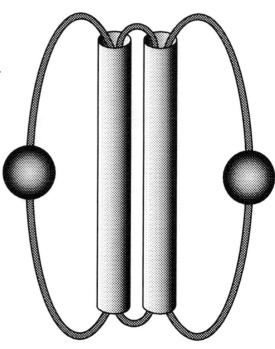

Making the Puzzle

1. Cut two 6" lengths of cardboard tube from a pants hanger.
2. Roll up a very small piece of sandpaper and sand the holes in two large beads to remove any rough edges.
3. Cut a 44" piece of thick string and seal the ends.
4. Double up the string twice so that one side has two loops and the other side has one loop and two loose ends.
5. Take the two loops that are on one side of the string and the two tubes. Push each loop through a tube until a little loop sticks out of the opposite end of the tube.
6. Put a bead on each loose end of the string.
7. Thread one loose end of the string through the loops sticking out of the ends of the tubes.
8. Tie the loose ends of the string together with a knot.
9. Pull the strings out of one end of each tube until the interlocking loops and the knot are hidden inside the tubes, as shown above.

Solving the Puzzle

Join the two beads on the same section of the string so that you have both beads on one section and none on the other. Once you've done that, separate the beads again. Always hide the knot and interlocking loops inside the tubes before challenging someone to solve this puzzle.

Puzzloop is a modification of a wood and string puzzle described in Nob Yoshigahara's book *Puzzle in Wood*. Instead of using wooden dowels and disks, we'll use cardboard tubes and plastic rings. The puzzle does not look as elegant, but it can easily be constructed with household items and does not require special materials or tools. In this puzzle, two identical pieces are interlocked with one another, as shown below. How do you take them apart? If you only think of the open loop principle, you are just half-way there, because the rings are a little too tight for the string to pass through when they are around the cardboard tubes.

Materials Required

- 1 cardboard tube from a pants hanger
- 12" of thick string
- 2 small rings
- ruler
- scissors

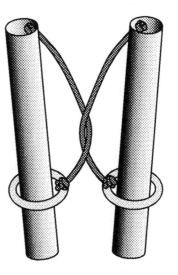

Making the Puzzle

1. Cut two 5" lengths of cardboard tube from a pants hanger.
2. Use a tip of the scissors to poke a small hole at one end of each of the tubes. The hole should be about $1/3$" from the edge of the tube's end.
3. Cut two 6" pieces of thick string and seal the ends.
4. Attach an end of each string to a small ring.
5. Slip a ring on a tube and thread the loose end of the string through the small hole in the tube. Tie a knot so that the end of the string will not pull out.
6. Slip the other ring around the other tube and thread the loose end of the string first through the other string and then through the small hole on the tube, as shown above.
7. Tie a knot at the end of the string so that it will not pull out.

Solving the Puzzle

Separate the two cardboard tubes. Once they are separated put them back together as in the initial state.

This simple puzzle is designed for beginning puzzle solvers. Here you have a cup with three holes. A string is threaded through two of the holes and both ends of the string are attached to small beads to lock the string there. There is a beaded string loop threaded through the other hole and the string loop is around the other string. Your objective is to remove the beaded string loop.

Materials Required

- 1 plastic or paper cup 3" high and 2" in diameter
- 9" of thick string
- 8" of thin string
- 3 small beads
- ruler
- scissors
- hole punch

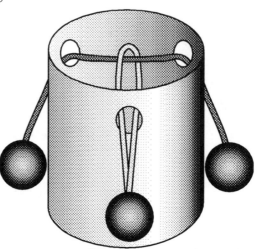

Making the Puzzle

1. You can either use a paper cup or cut a 3" high section from the bottom of a plastic bottle and smooth the cut edge with scissors or sandpaper. Make sure the material is not too thick to have holes punched in it.

2. Punch three holes ¹/₈" from the edge; they should be of equal distance from each other.

3. Cut an 8" piece of thin string and a 9" piece of thick string and seal the ends.

4. Double up the thin string and thread the doubled-up end through a small bead. Then tie a knot at the ends of the string and pull the bead back to cover up the knot tightly inside the hole.

5. Thread one loose end of the thick string through a small bead, tie a knot at the end of the string, and then pull the bead toward the knot until it covers the knot tightly inside its hole.

6. Thread the thick string and the beaded string loop through the holes in the cup, as shown above.

7. Finally, thread the remaining bead through the loose end of the string, tie a knot at the end, and pull the bead to cover the knot tightly inside its hole.

Solving the Puzzle

Remove the beaded string loop from the cup. Once you've done that, put it back again, as in the figure above.

Here we have a cup with a piece of string threaded through the cup's four holes. The string crosses itself inside the cup, forming a simple overhand knot. It is easy to see that there are three crossings in the knot. What would the string look like when the knot is untied? Do all the crossings disappear? Can you answer this question just by looking at the figure below?

Materials Required

- 1 plastic or paper cup 3" high and 2" in diameter
- 14" of thick string
- 2 small beads
- ruler
- scissors
- hole punch

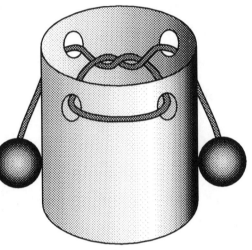

Making the Puzzle

1. You can either use a paper cup or cut a 3" high section from the bottom of a plastic bottle and smooth the cut edge with scissors or sandpaper. Make sure the material is not too thick to have holes punched in it.
2. Punch four holes 1/8" from the edge; they should be of equal distance from each other.
3. Cut a 14" piece of thick string and seal the ends.
4. Tie a knot close to one end of the string and thread a bead through the other end of the string. Pull the bead all the way toward the knot until it covers the knot tightly in its hole.
5. Thread the loose end of the string through the holes in the cup, as shown. Make sure that you have a knot inside the cup.
6. Thread the other bead onto the loose end of the string, tie a knot, and then pull the bead back to cover the knot tightly in its hole.

Solving the Puzzle

Untie the knot inside the cup. Once you have done that, tie a knot inside the cup, as shown above.

Cupped Ring

There are three holes in the cup. A string is hitched on one of the holes and the ends of the string are threaded through the other holes. A bead is attached to each end of the string so that the ends cannot pass through the holes. A ring is trapped around the string inside the cup. Can you take the ring out?

Materials Required

- 1 plastic or paper cup 3" high and 2" in diameter
- 15" of thick string
- 2 small beads
- 1 medium-sized ring
- ruler
- scissors
- hole punch

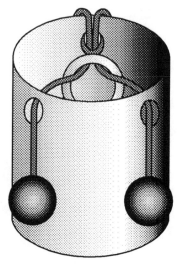

Making the Puzzle

1. You can either use a paper cup or cut a 3" high section from the bottom of a plastic bottle and smooth the cut edge with scissors or sandpaper. Make sure the material is not too thick to have holes punched in it.
2. Punch three holes ⅛" from the edge; they should be of equal distance from each other.
3. Cut a 15" piece of thick string and seal the ends.
4. Double up the string and push the doubled-up end through a hole in the cup to make a little loop inside the cup.
5. Thread the loose ends of the string first through the loop and then through the ring.
6. Thread each loose end of the string through the closest remaining hole and then through a bead.
7. Tie knots to stop the beads from coming off, then hide the knots by pulling them tightly inside the beads.

Solving the Puzzle

Remove the ring from the string. Once you get the ring off, put it back on again.

This puzzle is topologically equivalent to the puzzle *Cupped Loop.* Can you transform these two puzzles into one another? In this puzzle, a puzzleboard with three holes is used instead of a cup with three holes. A beaded string loop is threaded through the center hole of the puzzleboard, and it is locked in the puzzle by another string threaded through it. Can you remove the beaded string loop?

Materials Required

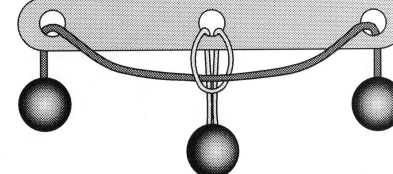

- 1 puzzleboard
- 10" of thick string
- 10" of thin string
- 3 small beads
- ruler
- scissors
- sandpaper

Making the Puzzle

1. Sand the holes in the puzzleboard to get rid of any rough edges.
2. Cut a 10" piece of thin string and a 10" piece of thick string and seal the ends.
3. Double up the thin string and thread the doubled-up end through a small bead. Then tie a knot at the ends of the string and pull the bead back to cover up the knot tightly inside the hole.
4. Thread one loose end of the thick string through a small bead, tie a knot at the end of the string, and then pull the bead toward the knot until it covers the knot tightly inside its hole.
5. Thread the thick string and the beaded string loop through the holes in the puzzleboard, as shown above.
6. Finally, thread the remaining bead through the loose end of the thick string, tie a knot at the end, and pull the bead to cover the knot tightly inside its hole.

Solving the Puzzle

Free the string loop from the rest of the puzzle. After you have freed the string loop, put it back on again.

Exploring Math Through Puzzles

This is a variation of some traditional puzzles that have an overhand knot in the string. As you can see, the string is threaded through the two end holes in the puzzleboard and the large bead. The ends of the string are attached to small beads to stop them from coming off the holes. An overhand knot is tied around the large bead in the center of the string. Your objective? Untie the knot, of course.

Materials Required

- 1 puzzleboard
- 14" of thick string
- 1 large bead
- 2 small beads
- ruler
- scissors
- sandpaper

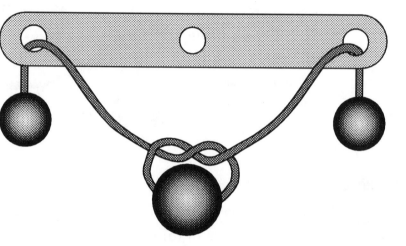

Making the Puzzle

1. Sand the holes in the puzzleboard and the large bead to get rid of any rough edges.

2. Cut a 14" piece of thick string and seal the ends.

3. Thread the string through the large bead and tie an overhand knot.

4. Thread both ends of the string through the two end holes in the puzzleboard, as shown above.

5. For each end of string, first thread a small bead, then tie a knot close to the end of the string, and finally pull the bead to cover the knot tightly inside its hole.

Solving the Puzzle

Untie the knot in the string. Once you've done that, tie a knot in the string again.

Hanging Loop

In this puzzle, a string loop is locked around two open loops formed by a beaded string together with a puzzleboard. Analyze the **open loops** to find a way to release the locked string.

Materials Required

- 1 puzzleboard
- 14" of thick string
- 10" of thin string
- 3 small beads
- ruler
- scissors
- sandpaper

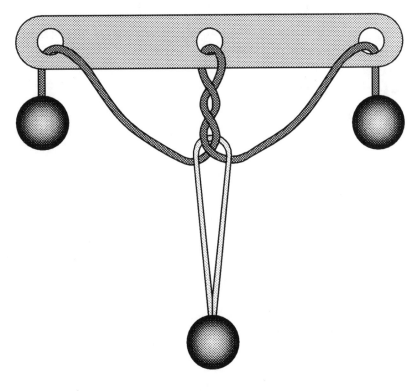

Making the Puzzle

1. Sand the holes in the puzzleboard to get rid of any rough edges.
2. Cut a 14" piece of thick string and a 10" piece of thin string and seal the ends.
3. Thread one end of the thick string through the center hole in the puzzleboard.
4. Then twist both ends of the string one and a half turns (the number of times the string is twisted does not really play any role in the puzzle at all), and thread each end through an end hole in the puzzleboard, as shown above.
5. Next, thread each end of the string through a small bead. Tie knots to prevent the beads from coming off, then hide the knots by pulling them tightly inside the beads.
6. Now loop the thin string around the twisted part of the thick string, as shown.
7. Thread both ends of the thin string through a small bead, tie the ends together with a knot, and pull the bead tightly over the knot.

Solving the Puzzle

Free the string loop from the rest of the puzzle. After you have freed the string loop, put it back on again.

Exploring Math Through Puzzles

A large bead is indeed trapped in a piece of string and the puzzleboard. Just looking at this puzzle in the figure below gives you no clue whether you can free the bead or how. The question you want to raise here is, "How is the string threaded inside the hole of the large bead?" Can you figure out some ways that the piece of string can be threaded through the large bead? How many are there? How should the string appear when the large bead is removed from the puzzle?

Materials Required

- 1 puzzleboard
- 18" of thick string
- 1 large bead
- 1 small bead
- ruler
- scissors
- sandpaper

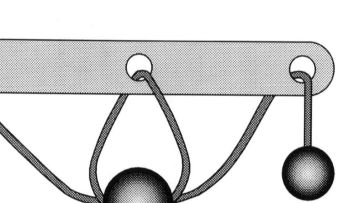

Making the Puzzle

1. Sand the holes in the puzzleboard and the large bead to get rid of any rough edges.

2. Cut an 18" piece of thick string and seal the ends.

3. Tie one end of the string to the end hole on the left of the puzzleboard.

4. Double up the string and thread the loop end of the string through the large bead.

5. Next thread the loose end of the string through the center hole from behind, then through the string loop, and finally through the other end hole on the right, as shown below.

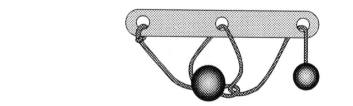

6. Finally, thread the small bead onto the loose end of the string, tie a knot close to the end, and pull the bead tightly over the knot.

Solving the Puzzle

Remove the trapped large bead from the rest of the puzzle. Once you've done that, put it back on again.

Hitched Knot

When a piece of string is looped into a knot with the help of another rigid object, such as a post or a ring, the knot is then **hitched** to that object. Here you have a string with one end tied to an end hole of a puzzleboard and the other end threaded through the center hole of the puzzleboard and then fastened to a bead. The middle of the string is hitched onto the other end hole of the puzzleboard and forms a square knot together with the hole. Your challenge is to untie the hitched knot. Beware: this is harder to do than it appears.

Materials Required

- 1 puzzleboard
- 20" of thick string
- 1 small bead
- ruler
- scissors
- sandpaper

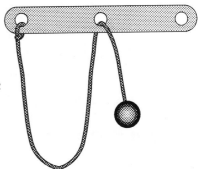

Making the Puzzle

1. Sand the holes in the puzzleboard to remove any rough edges.
2. Cut a 20" piece of thick string and seal the ends.
3. Double up the string and push the doubled-up end through one end hole in the puzzleboard to make a little loop.
4. Thread both loose ends of the string through the loop and tie one end to the hole on the other end of the puzzleboard.
5. Thread the other loose end of the string through the center hole of the puzzleboard and then through the small bead.
6. Tie a knot at the end of the string and pull the knot into the bead to secure it tightly inside.

Solving the Puzzle

Solve this puzzle by untying the square knot that is hitched to an end hole in the puzzleboard. Once the knot is gone (as shown at the right), see if you can tie it again.

This puzzle is composed of a puzzleboard (the yoke) with two string loops, each locked in one of the puzzleboard's end holes by a pair of beads. The two string loops are linked together with a square knot, which is covered by a large bead (the yoked bead) that has to be removed.

Materials Required

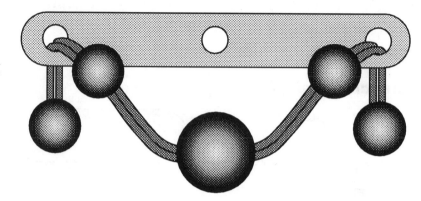

- 1 puzzleboard
- 24" of thick string
- 1 large bead
- 4 small beads
- ruler
- scissors
- sandpaper

Making the Puzzle

1. Roll up a very small piece of sandpaper and sand the holes in the puzzleboard and the large bead until they are smooth inside.
2. Cut two 12" pieces of thick string and seal the ends.
3. Now double up each string and thread the ends of one string through the loop of the other string to make a square knot, as shown here.

4. Thread either end of the doubled-up string through the large bead.
5. Now tie a knot in the center of the doubled-up string segment on each side. Then thread each doubled-up string through a small bead and pull the bead onto the knot to cover it up tightly. You may have to use a threading aid.
6. Thread one doubled-up string through one of the end holes in the puzzleboard and then through another small bead. Tie a knot at the end of the doubled-up string, and pull the bead onto the knot to cover it up tightly.
7. Repeat step 6 for the other doubled-up string. Now the strings should be locked onto the puzzleboard as shown, and the small beads should be fastened on the string too tightly to slide.

Solving the Puzzle

Remove the large bead from the puzzle: that is, untie the square knot in the center of the puzzle so that the large bead can be freed. After the large bead has been removed, then put it back on.

This puzzle is topologically equivalent to *Cupped Ring*. Instead of a cup, the ring is trapped on the puzzleboard (the yoke). If you closely examine how the string is hitched to the center hole in the puzzleboard, you will notice that the string together with the center hole form a square knot. The objective of this puzzle is to take the yoked ring off the puzzle. At first glance this might look impossible, because the ring is too large to pass through the holes in the puzzleboard. Will the ring come off if we untie the square knot? But how can you untie this square knot?

Materials Required

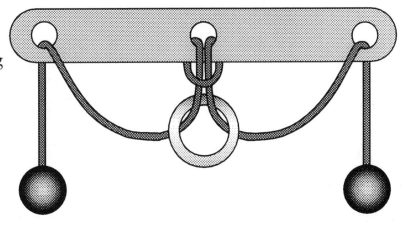

- 1 puzzleboard
- 20" of thick string
- 1 medium-sized ring
- 2 small beads
- ruler
- scissors
- sandpaper

Making the Puzzle

1. Sand the holes in the puzzleboard to make them smooth.
2. Cut a 20" piece of thick string and seal the ends.
3. Take the string and double it up.
4. Push the doubled-up end through the center hole in the puzzleboard to make a little loop.
5. Thread the loose ends of the string first through the loop and then through the ring.
6. Thread each loose end of the string through one end hole in the puzzleboard and then through a bead.
7. Tie knots to stop the beads from coming off, then hide the knots by pulling them tightly inside the beads.

Solving the Puzzle

Remove the ring from the string. Once you get the ring off, you'll face the challenge of putting it on again.

This is a modification of a classic Chinese puzzle called *The Imperial Scale*, which has a ring locked onto a string loop in the center of an ivory square suspended by a string at each of its four corners. If you know how to solve the *Yoked Ring* puzzle, you should be able to solve this one too. They are, after all, very similar topologically.

Materials Required

- 1 puzzleboard
- 14" of thick string
- 13" of thin string
- 3 small beads
- 1 small ring
- 1 large ring
- ruler
- scissors
- sandpaper

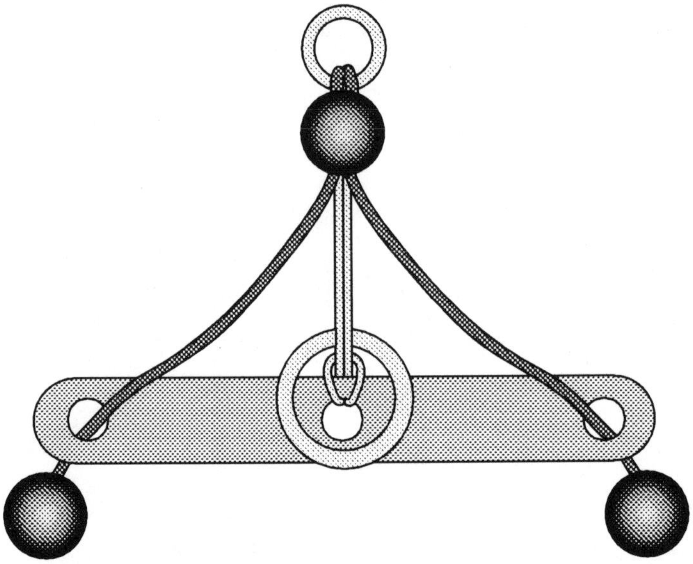

Making the Puzzle

1. Sand the holes in the puzzleboard until they are smooth.
2. Cut a 14" piece of thick string and a 13" piece of thin string and seal the ends.
3. Double up the thin string and thread the looped end through the center hole in the puzzleboard.
4. Thread the loose ends of the string first through the loop, then through the large ring, and finally through a small bead.
5. Tie the ends of the thin string with a knot.
6. Thread one end of the thick string through the loop with the knot. Double up the thick string and thread both ends first through a small ring and then through the bead already on the thin string (from the side next to the knot).
7. Arrange the strings so that the thick string passes the small ring for about 1/8" and the thin string loops around the thick string with the knot next to the crossing. Pull the bead toward the small ring to cover up the knot.
8. Thread each loose end of the thick string through one end hole in the puzzleboard and then through a small bead. Tie knots to stop the beads from coming off, then hide the knots tightly inside the beads.

Solving the Puzzle

Remove the large ring from the rest of the puzzle. Once it has been freed, put it back on as shown in the figure.

This puzzle has a long history in the Ivory Coast, Guinea, and other countries of West Africa. It is still popular among city dwellers as well as people living in outlying areas. The earliest versions of the puzzle were made from a straight branch or twig and threaded with vines woven to make a cord. Clay beads or stones, through which holes had been bored, were then added.

In China, this puzzle was constructed with materials ranging from wire, string, and old Chinese coins (which have a hole in the middle) to meticulously carved ivory bars and beads.

There are many versions of the *African Bead Puzzle*, but the objective is always to transfer a bead or ring from one hanging loop of cord to the other. The hole in the center of the bar is too small for the bead to pass through, so another way must be found.

Materials Required

- 1 puzzleboard
- 20" of thick string
- 2 large beads
- ruler
- scissors
- sandpaper

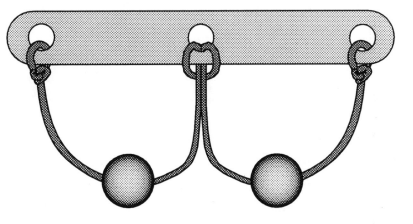

Making the Puzzle

1. Roll up a very small piece of sandpaper and sand the holes in the puzzleboard and in the two large beads to remove any rough edges.
2. Cut a 20" piece of thick string and seal the ends.
3. Double up the string and push the doubled-up end through the center hole in the puzzleboard to make a little loop.
4. Thread the loose ends of the string through the loop and put a bead on each loose end of the string.
5. Tie each loose end to a hole at one end of the puzzleboard, as shown above.

Solving the Puzzle

Get the two beads onto the same section of the string. When the beads are together, then you can challenge your friends to separate them.

This version of the *African Bead Puzzle* is complicated by the fact that both loops of the string pass through a common bead at the center. In Ivory Coast this puzzle is called *Kpa Kpa Powa* ("body of the parrot") and is made from bamboo, the fruit of the *bola kow* tree, and vine.

The objective is to transfer all the beads from one side of the center knot to the other. That large bead in the center seems to block the smaller beads from moving from one side to the other, but it actually adds very little complexity to the puzzle.

Materials Required

- 1 puzzleboard
- 25" of thick string
- 1 large bead
- 6 medium-sized beads
- ruler
- scissors
- sandpaper

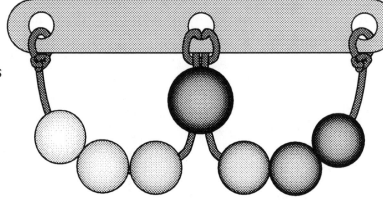

Making the Puzzle

1. Roll up a very small piece of sandpaper and sand the holes in the puzzleboard and in all the beads to remove any rough edges.
2. Cut a 25" piece of thick string and seal the ends.
3. Double up the string and push the doubled-up end through the center hole in the puzzleboard to make a little loop.
4. Thread the loose ends of the string first through the loop and then through the large bead. Then put three medium-sized beads on each loose end of the string.
5. Tie each loose end to a hole at one end of the puzzleboard.

Solving the Puzzle

Transfer all the medium-sized beads to one side of the string. Once they are all together, separate them into two groups of three again.

It is easy to see some similarity between this puzzle and *Hitched Knot*. This puzzle has three square knots instead of one, and, in addition, neither end of the string is tied to a hole. What do you think the objective of the puzzle is? If you understand *Hitched Knot* well enough, you should be able to tell that the beaded string can come completely off the puzzleboard.

Materials Required

- 1 puzzleboard
- 22" of thick string
- 2 small beads
- ruler
- scissors
- sandpaper

Making the Puzzle

1. Sand the holes in the puzzleboard to remove any rough edges.
2. Cut a 22" piece of thick string and seal the ends.
3. Double up the string. Push the doubled-up end through the center hole in the puzzleboard to make a little loop, and then thread both loose ends of the string through the loop.
4. Match each end of the string with the closest end hole in the puzzleboard. (It really doesn't matter if there is a mismatch, except the completed puzzle won't look as neat.) Then hitch each string end onto its corresponding end hole using a square knot, as shown.
5. Thread each string end through a bead, and then tie a knot at the end. Finally, pull the knot into the bead to secure it tightly inside.

Solving the Puzzle

Remove the beaded string from the puzzleboard. After you've removed it, then hitch it back on again.

Variation

If you enjoy challenges, you might like to explore what else you can do with this puzzle. How about trying to put it together so that there is a square knot at each end and both string ends are locked in the center hole of the puzzleboard?

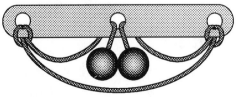

Exploring Math Through Puzzles

Here is a very interesting puzzle that can be made from a couple of beads and a piece of string. It was invented in 1992 by Christiaan Freeling and Anneke Treep of the Netherlands and has been sold under the Dutch name *Treiterkraaltjes*. The English translation is *Bugballs*. It is recommended that the beads be no smaller than 3/4" in diameter and that the string be thick for easy handling. Some commercial puzzles of this type are made of two rubber balls the size of a fist and heavy nylon cord.

Materials Required

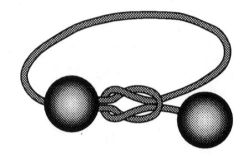

- 12" of thick string
- 2 small beads
- ruler
- scissors

Making the Puzzle

1. Cut a 12" piece of thick string and seal the ends.
2. Tie a loop at one end of the string just small enough so that a bead cannot pass through the loop.
3. Thread the loose end of the string through a bead, and pull the bead toward the loop until the knot is securely hidden inside the hole of the bead. Make sure that you do not pull the bead too far, making the loop too small.
   (In the original design, this bead is not fastened at all. It can slide freely between the loop and the bead at the other end of the string.)
4. Thread the loose end of the string through the loop to form a square knot, as shown above. You may want to leave a little extra room at the loose end of the string to finish the puzzle.
5. Thread the other bead onto the loose end of the string. Tie a knot at the end, and pull the bead back to hide the knot securely inside.

Solving the Puzzle

To solve the puzzle, you have to untie the square knot. Once it has been untied, you'll then have to tie it up again.

Variation:

After you've become an expert at solving this puzzle, try to "buttonhole" it on a friend. Don't you think it's more fun this way?

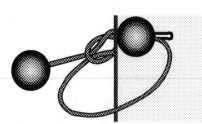

Legend has it that wire puzzles were invented as locks by Chinese farmers thousands of years ago. Over the years, they evolved into recreational novelties and have taken many different forms. The puzzle below is one of the simplest of its kind. The puzzle has two parts, an open loop (*A* and *B*) and a closed loop (*C*). *A* and *B* form an open loop because there are openings that allow an interlocked object to be freed from the loop. *C* is a closed loop because its ends are tightly fastened together. In the figure below, the closed loop is interlocked with the open loop. Can you unlock the loops?

Materials Required

- 23" of wire
- ruler
- pliers

Making the Puzzle

1. Cut a 5" length of wire to make *A*. Bend an end loop approximately ⁵/₈" in diameter at each end of the wire.

2. Cut an 8" length of wire to make *B*. First bend two ⁵/₈"-diameter end loops, but leave them open for now. Then bend the U-shape, making sure that the end loops are on planes perpendicular to that of the U-shape.

3. Lock *A* and *B* together by closing the end loops of *B* around *A*. The end loops of *B* are called locking loops because they are used to lock *A* in place.

> **Stop and Play:** Loop a 10" piece of thick string through the open loop formed by *A* and *B* and tie the ends together. Now try to remove the string. Once it is free, put it back on again. Take it off when you are ready to finish making the puzzle.

4. Cut a 10" length of wire to make *C*. First bend an eye (a small wire loop about ³/₈" in diameter) at each end of the wire, but leave them open for now. Then bend an indenting tongue in the center of the wire. It should be about ³/₄" long and no more than ¹/₄" wide. Form the rest of the shape, but do not lock the eyes together yet.

5. Loop piece *C* through the loop formed by *A* and *B*, and then lock the eyes of *C*.

Solving the Puzzle

Release the closed loop *C* from the rest of the puzzle. Once it is free, you can try to lock it on again.

Exploring Math Through Puzzles

This puzzle is topologically equivalent to *Heart Lock*, which is used as an example in the discussion of simple open loop puzzles in this book (page 17). The two puzzles are topologically equivalent because if one of the puzzles was made out of "rubber wire," you could twist, stretch, and bend it into the shape of the other puzzle. The difference between this puzzle and *Heart Lock* lies only in the shapes of the parts. In this puzzle, the locking loop of the square holds an end loop that points inward. That also determines which way the tongue of the arrow must point.

Materials Required

- 20" of wire
- ruler
- pliers

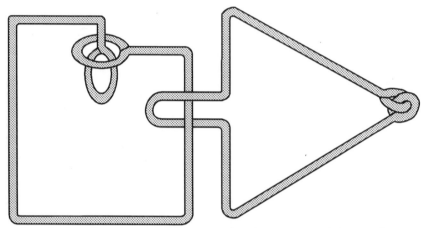

Making the Puzzle

1. Cut an 11" length of wire for the square. First make two end loops $5/8$" in diameter, but leave one of them open for now. Next twist the wire so that the two end loops are on the same plane. Then bend the wire to form a square, as shown above, with the closed end loop sticking inward through the open end loop. Finally, close the locking loop.

> **Stop and Play:** Loop a 10" piece of thick string through the square and tie the ends together. Now try to separate the string loop from the open loop of the square. Once it is free, put it back on again. Take it off when you are ready to finish making the puzzle.

2. Cut a 9" length of wire to make the arrow. First bend the eyes, but leave them open for now. Then bend the protruding tongue in the center, and make sure it is about $3/4$" long and no more than $1/4$" wide. Form the rest of the arrow, but do not lock the eyes together yet.

3. Interlock the arrow and the square as shown, and then lock the eyes together.

Solving the Puzzle

Release the arrow from the square. After the pieces have been separated, lock them back together again.

Variations

Create your own designs for the open and closed loops. Use a protruding tongue on your closed loop, and make sure your open loop locks inward.

California puzzle artist Rick Irby uses quality stainless steel to make *Double Crossed* and many other fascinating puzzles with intriguing original designs. This puzzle is almost the same as *Arrow Lock*—with an extra twist. If you know how to solve the previous lock puzzles, you shouldn't have too much trouble with this one.

Materials Required

- 25" of wire
- ruler
- pliers

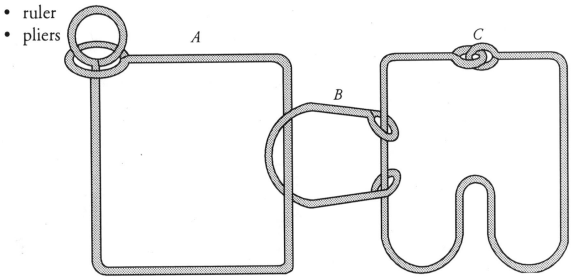

Making the Puzzle

1. Cut an 11" length of wire for *A*. First make a loop ⁵/₈" in diameter at each end of the wire, but leave one of the end loops open for now. Next, twist the wire so that the planes of the two end loops are perpendicular to each other. Then bend the wire to form a square, as shown above, with the closed end loop sticking through the open end loop. Do not close the open end loop yet.

2. Cut a 4" length of wire for *B*. First bend an eye at each end of the wire, making the eyes just large enough to freely slide on a straight piece of wire. Then bend the wire into the shape of *B* above, with the eyes bent inward at 45° angles.

3. Cut a 10" length of wire for *C*. First find the center of the wire and bend the indenting tongue, making sure it is about ³/₄" long and no more than ¹/₄" wide. Then form the rest of the shape, as shown above. Slide on *B* before making an eye at each end of *C* and locking them together. Make sure that *B* can slide freely on *C*.

4. Finally, interlock *A* and *B*, and then close the locking loop in *A*.

Solving the Puzzle

Release the square (open loop) from the other two pieces. After you've removed it, lock it back on again.

This puzzle is sold under many names in game and toy stores. It is a lock puzzle with a special feature. Since the two pieces in this puzzle are identical open loops, each piece must have an opening as well as a part that helps it pass through the opening. Can you identify these parts?

Materials Required

- 22" of wire
- ruler
- pliers

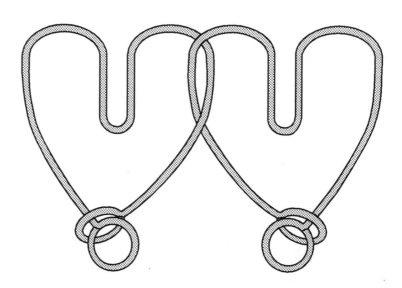

Making the Puzzle

1. Cut two 11" lengths of wire for the hearts.
2. Bend end loops on both wires, but leave one open on each wire for now. Each end loop should be about ⁵/8" in diameter.
3. For each wire, bend an indenting tongue in the center, making sure that it is about ³/4" long and no more than ¹/4" wide, and then form the heart. Twist the end loops so that the open end loop is on a plane perpendicular to that of the heart and the closed end loop. Finally, stick the closed end loop through the open end loop.
4. Interlock the hearts as shown and close each locking loop.

Solving the Puzzle

Unlock the hearts. Once you've done that, lock them back together again.

This is one of my original wire puzzle designs. Since the two pieces of this puzzle are identical, each piece has to contain both an open loop and a tongue that enables it to move in and out of the opening of the other piece's open loop. Can you identify these parts?

Materials Required

- 26" of wire
- 2 small rings
- ruler
- pliers

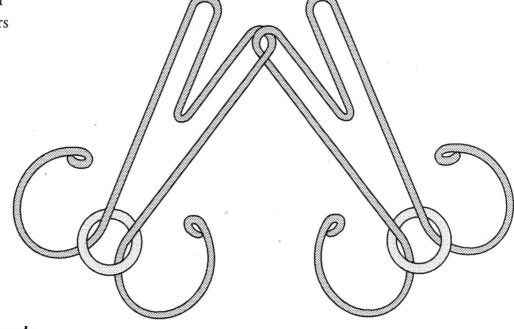

Making the Puzzle

1. Cut two 13" lengths of wire for the two scissors. Bend in both ends of each wire to hide the sharp end burrs.
2. Form a scissors shape by starting at the center of one of the wires and carefully bending it symmetrically toward both ends, as shown in the design. Slide in a small ring, and then form the handles of the scissors. The handles will secure the ring on the scissors.

> **Stop and Play:** Loop a 10" piece of thick string through the scissors and tie the ends together. Now try to take the string loop off the scissors. Once it is free, put it back on again. Take it off when you are ready to finish making the puzzle.

3. Repeat step 2 for the other scissors, but make sure that you interlock it with the finished scissors before sliding on the small ring and forming the handles.

Solving the Puzzle

Separate the two scissors. And once they are apart, link them back together again.

The name says it all. This puzzle looks just like a pair of old-fashioned eyeglasses with a string loop hanging from them. You can actually put it on your nose. What's so interesting about this simple puzzle is that trying to solve it can drive you crazy.

Materials Required

- 13" of wire
- 10" of thin string
- ruler
- pliers
- scissors

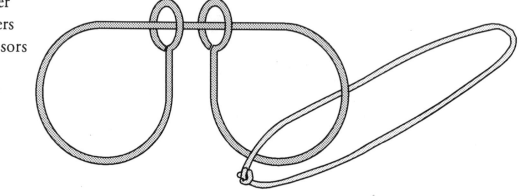

Making the Puzzle

1. Cut a 13" length of wire, and make a loop at each end, but do not close the loops yet. The diameter of each end loop should be around $^5/_8$".
2. Bend the wire to form the frame of the eyeglasses, as shown. Then close the two end loops.
3. Cut a 10" piece of thin string and seal the ends.
4. Thread the string through one side of the frame and tie the ends with a knot.

Solving the Puzzle

Remove the string loop from the eyeglasses. When it has been removed from the eyeglasses, put it back on again.

Figure 8   34

Some puzzles that look different from each other are topologically the same. This is the case with *Figure 8* and *Eyeglasses*. To see that they are topologically equivalent, just twist one loop of the 8 to the other side. Then you have a pair of eyeglasses. This puzzle will be easy for you—if you already know how to solve *Eyeglasses*.

Materials Required

- 13" of wire
- 10" of thin string
- ruler
- pliers
- scissors

Making the Puzzle

1. Cut a 13" length of wire, and make a loop at each end, but do not close the loops yet. The diameter of each loop should be around ⁵/8".
2. Form two larger loops in the wire as shown. Then close the small end loops.
3. Cut a 10" piece of thin string and seal the ends.
4. Thread the string through one of the large loops and tie the ends with a knot.

Solving the Puzzle

Remove the string loop from the *Figure 8*. When it has been removed, put it back on again.

At first glance this puzzle looks very much like *Figure 8*—yet there is a big difference. These two puzzles are not topologically equivalent, because you can't bend or twist one into the form of the other. You can try and try to remove the string loop from *Baffling 8*, but you'll only be baffled. Maybe you should stop and ask yourself, "Why?"

Materials Required

- 13" of wire
- 10" of thin string
- ruler
- pliers
- scissors

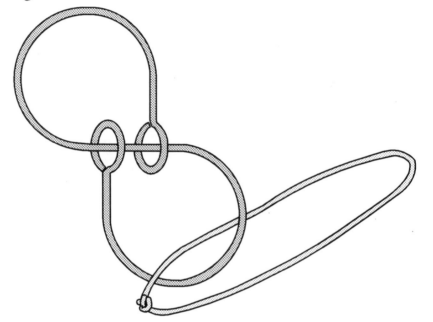

Making the Puzzle

1. Cut a 13" length of wire and make a loop at each end, but do not close the loops yet. The diameter of each loop should be around ⅝".
2. Form two larger loops in the wire, as shown. Then close the small end loops.
3. Cut a 10" piece of thin string and seal the ends.
4. Thread the string through one of the large loops and tie the ends with a knot.

Solving the Puzzle

Can you remove the string loop from the *Baffling 8* without cutting it? Why or why not?

This beautifully designed puzzle is made by Pentangle, one of the first companies devoted exclusively to producing puzzles. It looks complicated compared to the *Figure 8* puzzle. However, a closer look at these two puzzles reveals that they are topologically equivalent. Imagine this puzzle made of "rubber wire" so that it could be bent and twisted at will. Do you see how *Double Treble Clef* can be transformed into *Figure 8*?

Materials Required

- 23" of wire
- 10" of thick string
- ruler
- pliers
- scissors

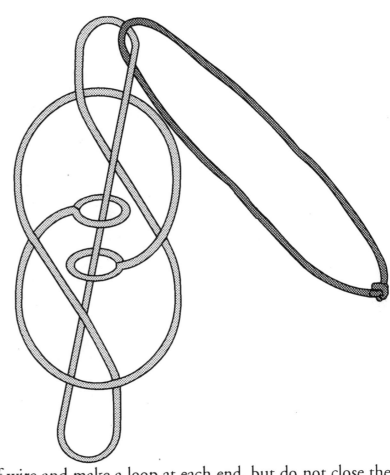

Making the Puzzle

1. Cut a 23" length of wire and make a loop at each end, but do not close the loops yet. The diameter of each loop should be around ⁵/8".
2. Mark a 4" segment in the center of the wire to leave straight. Starting from each end of this straight segment, bend the wire to form the shape shown above. Refer to the illustration very carefully with respect to whether the wire passes over or under the intersecting section of wire at each crossing.
3. Once the clef is formed, close the end loops.
4. Cut a 10" piece of thick string and seal the ends.
5. Thread the string through one of the large loops and tie the ends with a knot.

Solving the Puzzle

Remove the string loop from the clef. After you've taken it off, then put it back on again.

Looking at this puzzle, one cannot help wondering if it is topologically equivalent to *Double Treble Clef* on the previous page. Actually, they are two very different puzzles. Imagine this puzzle made of "rubber wire" so that it could be bent and twisted at will. If you held the puzzle by the two end loops and pulled them away from each other, you would end up with a straight piece of wire between the two end loops. (Can you visualize this?) This is not the case for *Double Treble Clef*. What would you get if you tried to "stretch out" *Double Treble Clef*? Experiment with a long piece of string.

Materials Required

- 23" of wire
- 10" of thick string
- ruler
- pliers
- scissors

Making the Puzzle

1. Cut a 23" length of wire and make a loop at each end, but do not close the loops yet. The diameter of each loop should be around ⁵/₈".

2. Mark a 4" segment in the center of the wire to leave straight. Starting from each end of this straight segment, bend the wire to form the shape shown above. Refer to the illustration very carefully with respect to whether the wire passes over or under the intersecting section of wire at each crossing.

3. Once the clef is formed, close the end loops.

4. Cut a 10" piece of thick string and seal the ends.

5. Thread the string through one of the large loops and tie the ends with a knot.

Solving the Puzzle

Remove the string loop from the clef. Once it is off, then put it back on again.

MATHEMATICS DEPARTMENT
ALVERNO COLLEGE
MILWAUKEE, WI 53234-3922

Compare this puzzle to *Double Treble Clef* and *Straight Clef*. At first you may think that it's more like *Straight Clef*, but actually it's very different. Even though *Trouble Clef* does not appear to be like *Double Treble Clef*, these two puzzles are topologically equivalent. To see this, use the "rubber wire" approach, and slide *Trouble Clef*'s end loops toward the midpoint of the wire. Once they get there, what do you have? Another *Double Treble Clef*.

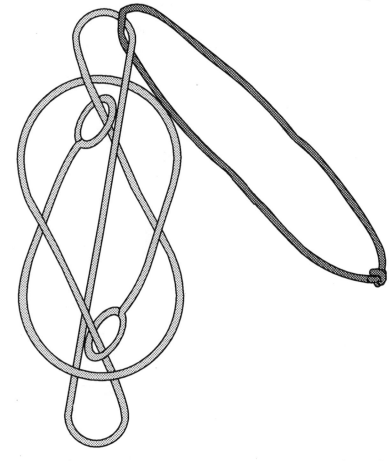

Materials Required

- 23" of wire
- 10" of thick string
- ruler
- pliers
- scissors

Making the Puzzle

1. Cut a 23" length of wire and make a loop at each end, but do not close the loops yet. The diameter of each loop should be around ⁵/₈".
2. Mark a 4" segment in the center of the wire to leave straight. Starting from each end of this straight segment, bend the wire to form the shape shown above. Refer to the illustration very carefully with respect to whether the wire passes over or under the intersecting section of wire at each crossing.
3. Once the clef is formed, close the end loops.
4. Cut a 10" piece of thick string and seal the ends.
5. Thread the string through one of the large loops and tie the ends with a knot.

Solving the Puzzle

Remove the string loop from the clef. Once it is off, put it back on again.

The symbol on the right is *Yin-yang*. It is the essence of *I Ching*, the Chinese *Book of Changes*. *Yin-yang* has many profound meanings in Chinese philosophy and culture. *Yin*, the dark part, is associated with the female principle, and *yang*, the light part, is associated with the male principle. Together *Yin-yang* represents harmony and ultimate unity. The shape of *Yin-yang* has long been used for mathematical problems involving geometric dissection. I designed this puzzle because of the intriguing shape of *Yin-yang*. It is a rather simple puzzle to solve.

Materials Required

- 16" of wire
- 10" of thick string
- 1 small bead
- 2 small rings
- ruler
- pliers
- scissors

Making the Puzzle

1. Cut a 16" length of wire. Start at the center of the wire and bend toward each end to form the shape above. Do not make the end loops yet.

2. From one end of the wire, slide two small rings to the center of the *Yin-Yang*.

3. Slide the rings apart and then back over the ends of the wire, as shown.

4. Bend a loop at each end of the wire. Make sure that the loops are large enough to keep the rings from sliding over them.

5. Cut a 10" piece of thick string and seal the ends.

6. Loop the string around the center of the *Yin-Yang*, as shown, and thread both ends through the bead. Tie the ends of the string together with a knot, and then pull the looped end until the knot is tightly hidden inside the bead.

Solving the Puzzle

Remove the string loop from the *Yin-Yang*. Once you've taken it off, put it back on again.

Here is a puzzle with a nested open loop structure. The two end loops are used to lock part of the wire inside them, and at the same time, they form the openings in the nested open loops. Let's use the "rubber wire" approach to see how the loops are nested. Use your imagination to "shrink" the bulb down to the size of a regular end loop. Now it is easy to see that the end loop around the bulb opens to the outside of the puzzle, and the open loop structure (the left part of the base) formed with this end loop is the outer loop. The other end loop at the bottom of the base opens only to the inside of the outer loop; therefore, it forms the inner loop (the right part of the base and the bulb) in this nested loop structure. There is a string loop locked in the inner loop of the *Light Bulb*. How do you remove it from the puzzle?

Materials Required

- 10" of thick string
- 16" of wire
- ruler
- pliers
- scissors

Making the Puzzle

1. Cut a 16" length of wire for the light bulb. Make an end loop at each end of the wire, but do not close them yet.
2. Next form the rectangular part of the light bulb, and then the round part. It doesn't matter if the rectangular part is a little larger or smaller than shown as long as you can lock the wire together with the end loops.
3. Close the loops as shown after the light bulb has been formed.
4. Cut a 10" piece of thick string and seal the ends.
5. Thread the string around the wire passing through the rectangular part of the light bulb, and tie the ends of the string together with a knot.

Solving the Puzzle

Remove the string loop from the light bulb. After you've removed it, put it back on again.

Variation

Attach a bead to the string loop (as in *Yin-Yang*) so that the string cannot pass through the end loops completely. Now try to solve the puzzle by taking the beaded string loop off the light bulb, and once it is off, put it back on again.

Exploring Math Through Puzzles

This is a simplified version of the *Butterfly Ring Puzzle* described in the *Ingenious Ring Puzzle Book* by Chong-En Yu and published in Shanghai, China, in 1958. In our version we have replaced the puzzle's wire handle with a loop of string. This puzzle is one of my personal favorites because of its beautiful design. *Butterfly* is not easy to make, but it is well worth the effort if you can do it.

Materials Required

- 28" of wire
- 10" of thick string
- 1 small bead
- 1 small ring
- ruler
- pliers
- scissors

Making the Puzzle

1. Cut a 20" length of wire for the butterfly. Start from the center of the wire and bend toward both ends, carefully following the figure above. After the butterfly has been formed, squeeze the two wings together so that you can slip the small ring over the butterfly's antennae.

2. Cut an 8" length of wire for the butterfly's hanger. Bend the end loops first, but don't close them yet. Finish forming the hanger. Then close the loops around the butterfly's wings.

3. Cut a 10" piece of thick string and seal the ends.

4. Loop the string around the hanger and then thread both ends through the bead. Tie the ends of the string together with a knot. Finally, pull the bead back to hide the knot securely inside.

Solving the Puzzle

Remove the string loop from the puzzle. After you've taken it off, put it back on again.

Here is another example of nested loop structure. The *Double Trapeze* puzzle works on the same principle as the *Chinese Rings* puzzle. In fact, the *Chinese Rings* can be thought of as a series of "half" trapezes linked together to form a nested structure.

This puzzle is made of two U-shaped pieces and one straight piece—forming a nested loop structure. Can you identify the outer loop and the inner loop?

Materials Required

- 18" of wire
- 10" of thick string
- ruler
- pliers
- scissors

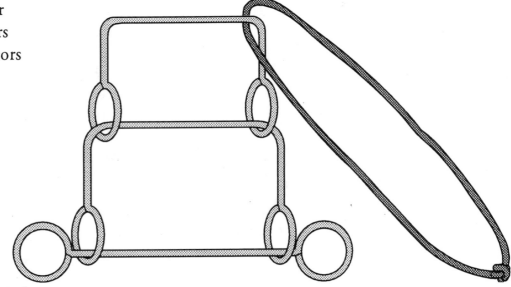

Making the Puzzle

1. Cut a 5" length of wire to make the straight piece. Close the end loops.
2. Cut 6" and 7" lengths of wire for the two U-shapes.
3. First bend the end loops, but do not close them yet. Then bend the wires into U-shapes, as shown above.
4. Link the U-shapes together as shown and close the locking end loops.
5. Cut a 10" piece of thick string and seal the ends.
6. Thread the string through the inner loop as shown and tie a knot.

Solving the Puzzle

Remove the string loop from the puzzle. When you've done that, put it back on again so that it is looped around the inner loop, as shown above.

Variation

When you become comfortable solving the puzzle, add one more U-shape to make a total of three nested loops. The new U-shape will form the innermost loop. Put the string loop on and off the innermost loop.

This puzzle shows how two puzzles based on the same principle can take very different forms. *"W"* is very much like the wire *Double Trapeze* puzzle, except that it is made of a string U-shape together with a wire one. In fact, we can even make U-shaped puzzles entirely out of string! As you can see, the inner loop (made out of wire) is locked by the string, and the outer loop (the string loop) is locked by a small ring.

By the way, have you deciphered this puzzle's name yet?

Materials Required

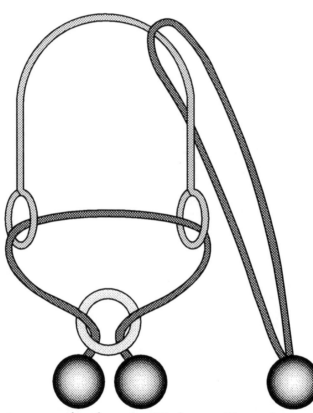

- 8" of wire
- 19" of thick string
- 3 small beads
- 1 small ring
- ruler
- pliers
- scissors

Making the Puzzle

1. Cut an 8" length of wire to make the wire U-shape. Close the end loops.
2. Cut 9" and 10" lengths of string and seal the ends.
3. Use the 9" string for the string U-shape. First thread it through the wire end loops, and then thread both ends through a small ring. Next thread each end of the string through a bead, tie a knot on the end, and pull the knot inside the hole of the bead to secure it there.
4. Use the 10" string to make the beaded string loop. First thread it through the wire U-shape, and then thread both ends of the string through a bead. Tie the ends together with a knot, and pull the knot inside the hole of the bead to secure it there.

Solving the Puzzle

Remove the beaded string loop from the rest of the puzzle. When it is free from the puzzle, lock it back around the wire U-shape.

Here is a challenging puzzle for you. You've got a ring locked around the string of *Big 4*. One end of the string is tied to the 4's stem, and the other end of the string is fastened to a bead that's too big to pass through the ring. How can you get the ring off the string?

Materials Required

- 9" of wire
- 8" of thick string
- 1 small ring
- 1 small bead
- ruler
- scissors
- pliers

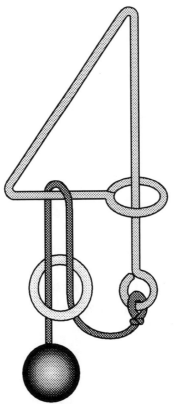

Making the Puzzle

1. Cut an 9" length of wire. Then bend a $^5/_8$"-diameter loop at one end of the wire and a $^3/_8$"-diameter eye at the other end, and leave the larger end loop open for now.
2. Bend the wire into the figure 4 as shown, and make sure that the plane of the larger end loop is perpendicular to the plane of the 4. Close the end loop around the stem of the 4.
3. Cut an 8" piece of thick string and seal the ends.
4. Tie one end of the string to the eye of the wire.
5. Thread the loose end of the string through the ring, through the triangle of the 4, back through the ring again, and finally through the small bead.
6. Tie a knot at the end of the string. Then hide the knot by pulling it tightly inside the bead.

Solving the Puzzle

Free the ring from the puzzle. Once it is free, put it back on again.

If we link two *4*'s together by their stems, we get a structure that can be deformed into an arch-shape with two small rectangular doors. The doors under the arch are too small to allow the beads to pass through. But we want to free the beaded string. Don't try to bend the doors to make them larger. That will spoil the challenge of the puzzle. Surely there is another way for the beaded string to get out.

Materials Required

- 14" of wire
- 10" of thick string
- 2 small beads
- ruler
- scissors
- pliers

Making the Puzzle

1. Cut a 14" length of wire, and bend each end into a loop ⁵⁄₈" in diameter. Leave both loops open for now.
2. Bend each end of the wire into a small rectangle on a plane perpendicular to that of the end loop. Make sure that the rectangles are not large enough for the beads to pass through. Close the end loops, as shown.
3. Bend the wire into the form of an arch.
4. Cut a 10" piece of thick string and seal the ends.
5. Thread the string through the rectangles, as shown.
6. Thread each end of the string through a bead, tie a knot at the end, and pull the bead back to hide the knot securely inside the hole.

Solving the Puzzle

Remove the beaded string from the arch. Once you've done that, put it back on again.

Variation

Need a challenging variation? Get a small ring and lock it onto the beaded string, as shown on the right.

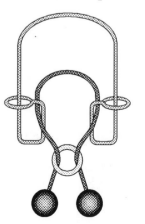

If you compare this puzzle with *Big 4*, you will see that their wire parts have exactly the same topological structure. However, the difference in the shapes of the locking loops makes these two puzzles completely different from each other. In this puzzle, the small ring cannot only slide in and out of the locking end loop, but it can also slide over the locking end loop! Enough said.

Materials Required

- 10" of wire
- 9" of thick string
- 1 small ring
- 1 small bead
- ruler
- scissors
- pliers

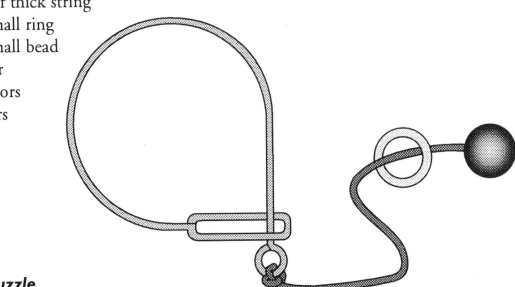

Making the Puzzle

1. Cut a 10" length of wire and bend one end into a ³/8" eye.
2. Bend the other end of the wire into a round-cornered rectangular loop that is large enough for the ring to slide through, but also narrow enough for the ring to slide over.
3. Twist the wire so that the planes of the two loops are perpendicular to each other. Bend the center part of the wire into three quarters of a circle and stick the end with the eye through the rectangular loop as shown.
4. Cut a 9" piece of thick string and seal the ends.
5. Thread one end of the string through a bead, tie a knot at the end, and pull the knot back into the bead to hide it securely.
6. Thread the other end of the string through the ring, and then tie the end to the eye of the wire.

Solving the Puzzle

Remove the ring from the puzzle. Once you've done that, put it back on again.

Exploring Math Through Puzzles

This puzzle is frequently made out of two real horseshoes connected together at their ends by small iron chains. A third horseshoe with its ends linked together is then looped around the chains. Horseshoe puzzles are very old, and they are still very popular. In our puzzle, the two connected horseshoes have been replaced by wire circles linked together with small rings, and the looped horseshoe by a large ring. Our puzzle works in the same way, but it's much easier to make.

Materials Required

- 16" of wire
- 1 large ring
- 2 small rings
- ruler
- pliers

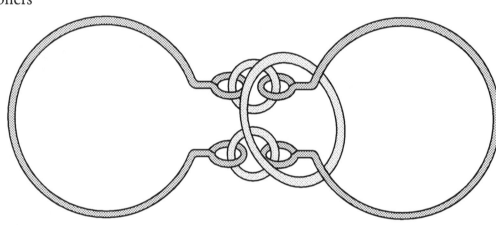

Making the Puzzle

1. Cut two 8" lengths of wire and bend an eye at each end. Make each eye just large enough to loosely hold a small ring. Do not close the eyes yet.
2. Bend each wire into a circle with an opening at the end, as shown above. Then twist the eyes so that they are on a plane perpendicular to the plane of the circles.
3. Lock a small ring onto each eye of one shackle. Then place a large ring around both ends of this shackle.
4. Now link the two halves of the puzzle by locking the eyes of the other shackle onto the two small rings.

Solving the Puzzle

Free the large ring from the shackles. Then put it back on again.

An earlier version of this puzzle was invented by Bowen E. Clarkson in 1904. A ring is locked in the center of four connected wire pieces. It can slide freely over the center pieces, but the end pieces are large enough to keep the ring from sliding off. As its name implies, there is a trick to freeing the ring from the *Fooler*—so be patient and you'll solve it!

Materials Required

- 26" of wire
- 1 large ring
- ruler
- pliers

Making the Puzzle

1. Cut two 6" and two 7" lengths of wire.
2. Use the 6" wires for the center pieces of the puzzle (the bars). First form eyes at the ends of the wire pieces, but leave the eyes open on one wire. Then bend each piece into a U-shaped bar narrow enough to fit through the large ring. Finally, twist the eyes so that the closed eyes are on the same plane as the bar they are on and the open eyes are on a plane perpendicular to the bar they are on.
3. Lock the eyes of the two bars together to form a hinge.
4. Now use the 7" wires for the end pieces of the puzzle (the sliding arches). Form eyes at the ends of these wire pieces and leave them open. These eyes must be large enough to allow the arches to slide along the bars.
5. Bend each piece into the shape of an arch, as shown. Twist the eyes so that each eye is on a plane perpendicular to that of the arch it is on. Make sure that each arch is too wide to fit through the large ring.
6. Attach a sliding arch to one of the bars as shown and close the eyes. Slide a large ring onto the other bar, attach the remaining sliding arch to it, and, finally, close the eyes. Make sure that the arches can slide on the bars.

Solving the Puzzle

Free the large ring from the *Fooler*. After it has been freed, put it back on again.

A hand-forged version of this puzzle was made in the late eighteenth or early nineteenth century and called the *Old Hinged Metal Puzzle*. Today it is sold by manufacturers of old-fashioned ironwork puzzles. Uncle's Puzzles of Maple Valley, Washington, sells this puzzle as *Gingerbread Man*, while Tucker-Jones House of Setauket, New York, calls its version *Conestoga Playmate* in its Tavern Puzzles Collection. Puzzles of this type were traditionally forged by blacksmiths to amuse their friends at country taverns and inns.

Materials Required

- 20" of wire
- 1 large ring
- ruler
- pliers

Making the Puzzle

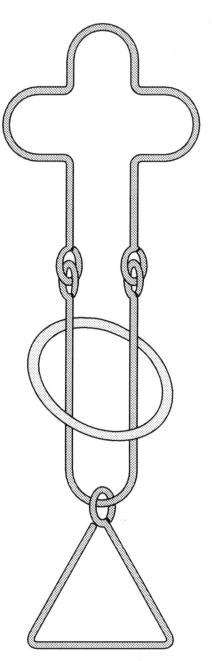

1. Cut 9", 6", and 5" lengths of wire.
2. Use the 9" wire to make the cross. First bend an eye at each end, and then form the cross, as shown. Make sure the eyes and the cross are on the same plane.
3. Bend an eye at each end of the 6" wire, but do not close them yet. Next bend this piece into a U-shaped bar so that the eyes are on a plane perpendicular to the plane of the bar.
4. Lock the eyes of the cross together with the the eyes of the bar to form a hinge.
5. Bend an eye at one end of the 5" wire, but leave it open for now. Then bend the rest of the wire into an equilateral triangle whose plane is perpendicular to the plane of the eye.
6. Slip the large ring onto the bar. Then loosely lock the eye of the triangle onto the curved part of the bar, as shown.

Solving the Puzzle

Remove the large ring from *The Cross*. After it has been freed, put it back on again.

Lyon's Loops is sold in many toy and game stores. It is rather easy to solve. We're not sure if the puzzle got its name from the two large loops that Lyon designed, which are mirror images of each other, or from Lyon's face, which some people claim to see in the puzzle. Each loop has straight ends that extend about 1" in both directions from their crossing point. The ends of the two loops are connected with small rings. A triangle hangs from one of these small rings with a large ring trapped on it. Your job is to free the large ring from the puzzle, but the triangle and the large loops are in the way.

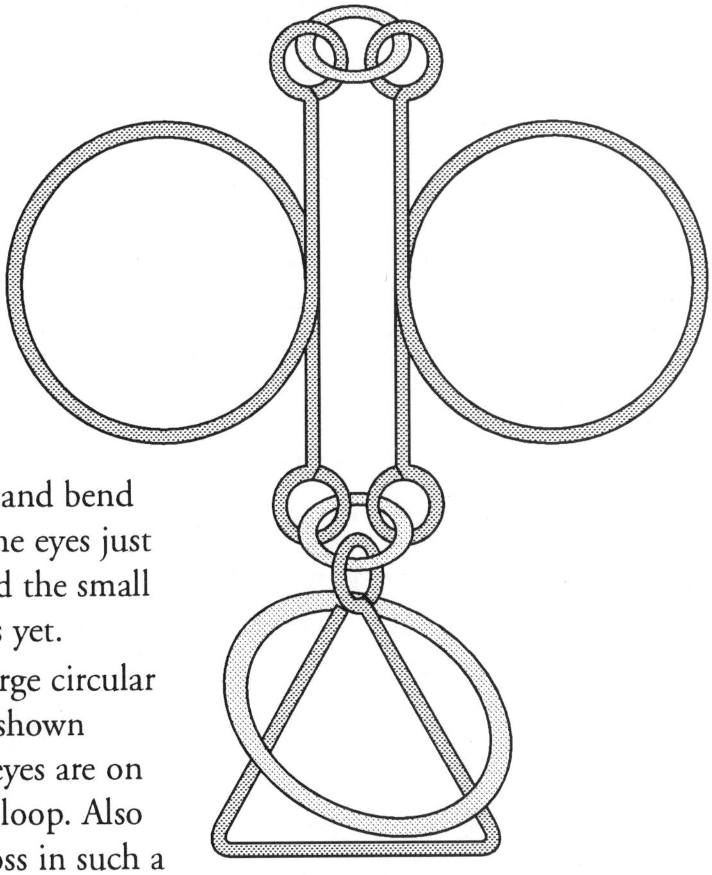

Materials Required

- 23" of wire
- 1 large ring
- 2 small rings
- ruler
- pliers

Making the Puzzle

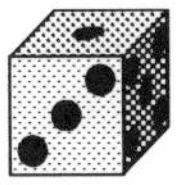

1. Cut two 9" lengths of wire and bend an eye at each end. Make the eyes just large enough to loosely hold the small rings. Do not close the eyes yet.

2. Bend each 9" wire into a large circular loop with straight ends, as shown above. Make sure that the eyes are on the same plane as the large loop. Also make sure that the ends cross in such a way that the two large loops are mirror images of each other.

3. Join the two large loops by closing a pair of eyes around each small ring, as shown.

4. Cut a 5" length of wire and bend an eye at one end. Leave it open for now. Then bend the rest of the wire into an equilateral triangle whose plane is perpendicular to the plane of the eye.

5. Place the large ring over the eye of the triangle, and then loosely lock the eye onto either of the small rings, as shown.

Solving the Puzzle

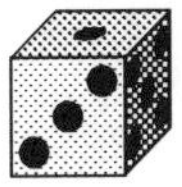

Remove the large ring from *Lyon's Loops*. After it has been freed, put it back on again.

Exploring Math Through Puzzles

Here are a lot of triangles indeed. The two main parts of the puzzle are mirror images of each other. These two parts are linked together at their ends by two small rings. Attached to one side of the puzzle is a small equilateral triangle with a large ring trapped between it and the main part of the puzzle. It looks impossible for the large ring to be freed from the rest of the puzzle. But that is the challenge.

Materials Required

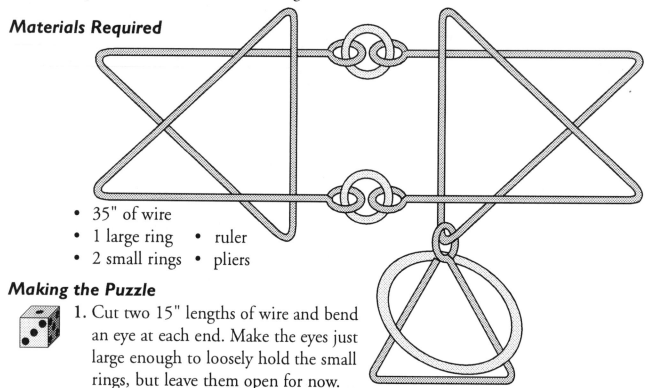

- 35" of wire
- 1 large ring   • ruler
- 2 small rings   • pliers

Making the Puzzle

1. Cut two 15" lengths of wire and bend an eye at each end. Make the eyes just large enough to loosely hold the small rings, but leave them open for now.

2. Divide each wire into five equal lengths, and make a small mark or bend at each point of division. Then form each wire into a double triangle, as shown. Pay attention to whether the wire is supposed to pass over or under the intersecting wire at each crossing.

3. Twist the eyes so that they are on a plane perpendicular to that of the double triangles. Link the two double triangles by locking both of them to two small rings as shown.

4. Cut a 5" length of wire and bend an eye at one end. Make the eye just large enough to slide freely on a wire, but leave it open for now. Then bend the rest of the wire into an equilateral triangle whose plane is perpendicular to the plane of the eye.

5. Place the large ring over the eye of the equilateral triangle, and then loosely lock the eye onto either one of the double triangles.

Solving the Puzzle

Remove the large ring from *Triangular Trickery*. After it has been freed, put it back on again.

Snail

Ishi Press in California sells a German-made version of this puzzle with a French name, *L'escargot*. It is a very interesting puzzle that can baffle even puzzle experts. The snail is really a wire loop that has been twisted 360° to form two loops, which are then folded together. Try to understand this by playing with a string loop. The center loop is made just small enough so that a small bead cannot pass through.

Materials Required

- 16" of wire
- 10" of thick string
- 2 small beads
- ruler
- scissors
- pliers

Making the Puzzle

1. Cut a 16" length of wire and bend an eye at each end of the wire. Leave one of the eyes open for now.
2. Form the wire into the snail, as shown. Be careful how the wire passes at the crossings. Also, make sure that the small loop and the opening in between the large and small loops are too small for a bead to pass through.
3. Connect the eyes and lock them together.
4. Cut a 10" piece of thick string and seal the ends.
5. Thread one end of the string through a bead, tie a knot at the end, and pull the knot securely inside the hole of the bead.
6. Thread the loose end of the string through the center loop of the snail and then through the other bead. Tie a knot at the end and pull it securely inside the hole of the bead.

Solving the Puzzle

Remove the beaded string from the snail. Once you've done that, put it back on again, as shown above.

Variation

A more challenging puzzle is made by locking a small ring on the string, as shown on the right.

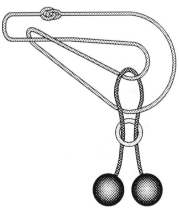

Exploring Math Through Puzzles

This is a wire version of a wood puzzle called *Wit's End*. In this puzzle a ring is trapped in the center of a wire frame. One end of the frame is too large for the ring to pass through; the other end is small enough but has a string loop passing through its center slot. Each end of the string has been threaded through a bead and tied to a ring. The trapped ring can pass over the beads, but not over the rings at the ends of the string. The rings attached to the ends of the string can pass through the center slot of the wire frame, but the beads cannot. Is there a way out for the trapped ring?

Materials Required

- 12" of wire
- 8" of thick string
- 3 medium-sized rings
- 1 small ring
- 2 small beads
- ruler, scissors, and pliers

Making the Puzzle

1. Cut a 12" length of wire and bend an eye at each end. Make sure the eyes are just large enough to loosely hold the small ring. Don't close them yet.

2. Starting from the center, form the wire part of the puzzle as shown. Close the eyes after the small ring is locked inside them.

3. Cut an 8" piece of thick string and seal the ends.

4. Tie a medium-sized ring onto one end of the string and thread the other end of the string through a bead.

5. Slide another medium-sized ring onto the center part of the wire, and then thread the loose end of the string through the slot in the center part of the wire, as shown above.

6. Thread the loose end of the string through the other bead, then tie it to the last ring.

Solving the Puzzle

Take off the ring trapped in the center of the puzzle. Once it is removed, put it back on again.

Variation

Remake the puzzle by looping the string through the center slot, as shown on the right. Now try to remove the trapped ring.

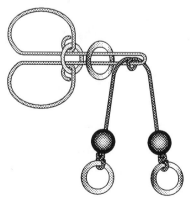

This is a classic Chinese puzzle of ingenuity, which is still popular in Chinese households. According to an old story, this puzzle was invented by the famous Chinese hero Hung Ming (A.D. 181–234), who gave it to his wife when he went off to war. The story relates that she forgot her sorrow while attempting to solve it. The *Chinese Rings* test your understanding of its underlying mathematical principle and your ability to devise a systematic procedure to solve it. It is also a classic example of nested structures. It can be constructed with as few as three rings up to any number you wish. However, you are advised not to build this puzzle with too many rings—if you want to solve it in your lifetime! Commercially available *Chinese Rings* often have nine rings. Shown here is a five-ring version. The ring on the left is the outermost and the ring on the right the innermost.

Materials Required

- 32" of wire
- 1 small bead
- 1 ring board with 5 holes
- 5 medium-sized rings
- ruler
- pliers

Making the Puzzle

1. Cut five 4" lengths of wire to make the ring holders. Bend one end of each wire to form an eye just large enough to loosely hold a ring. Put a ring into each eye, and then close it.

2. Cut a 12" length of wire for the handle. Make the handle narrow enough to go through the rings freely. Push both ends of the wire through the bead and then bend them apart and into two small loops to secure the bead in the handle.

3. Thread a ring holder through the handle and push it through the rightmost hole in the board. Then bend a small loop on the end of the ring holder to prevent it from coming out of the hole.

4. For the rest of the holes, moving from right to left, thread a ring holder first through the ring to its right and then through the corresponding hole in the board before bending a small loop to prevent it from coming out of the hole. Note that you can stop and play with three-ring and four-ring puzzles before you complete this five-ring puzzle.

Solving the Puzzle

Remove the handle from the puzzle. After you've done that, put the handle back on again so that it is locked by the innermost ring holder.

Designing Your Own Puzzles

Once you have made some puzzles and explored their mathematical principles, it's time to make some of your own puzzles. You can design a new puzzle in many different ways. Here we offer a few design guidelines for your own creations.

Adding Creative Touches

The simplest way to enhance a puzzle is to add a few creative touches to it. Some of the puzzles are made with puzzleboards, which can be decorated with artistic imagination. On the other hand, you can also modify the shapes and structures of some puzzles to make them more visually attractive. For example, the *African Bead Puzzle* contains a puzzleboard and two large beads; by adding a theme to it, you can redesign it as an airplane-shaped puzzleboard with two parachutes for the beads, or a ruler with two erasers. The wire puzzles offer a great possibility for your creative talent too. How about modifying the shapes and structures of some puzzles to make them more interesting?

When modifying existing puzzles or creating puzzles based on existing ones, be sure that you understand the mathematical principle behind these puzzles and what the maximum/minimum lengths and dimensions of parts of the puzzles must be. For example, if your own wire creation uses the open loop principle, and consists of an open loop and a closed loop, you will have to decide on the shape of the tongue, as well as the size of the opening end loop in the open loop. *Cupid's Lock*, below, is an example of the open loop principle.

Becoming Puzzle Inventors

Want to create original puzzles? Well, perhaps there is a potential puzzle inventor in you. It takes hard work, a lot of experience, and most of all, an open mind and plenty of imagination. There are many books available that you can read to expand your horizon in the world of puzzles. You'll find a good selection in the Bibliography, on page 119.

Activities — How to Use the Activities

This section contains a set of 12 activities for classroom and individual use. When using the activities in the classroom, it is best if the students work in small groups.

Puzzle-Making Activities

Activities 1, 2, and 3 are designed to help organize puzzle-making workshops. Each activity consists of 15 puzzles grouped according to the generalized difficulty level of their construction—easy, moderate, or hard. You might want to start with easy puzzles and move on to those that are more challenging.

If possible, have the students play with some already-made puzzles before they begin to construct their own. This always proves rewarding. You can guide their play by asking them to figure out the objective of each puzzle and challenging them to solve the puzzles. When working with young children, try to let them choose the puzzles they want to (or can) make. They will show a much stronger commitment if they make their own choices.

One way of using the card activity sheets is to highlight with a marker the puzzles that you intend each group to make, and then hand an activity sheet to each group and let each member of the group choose a puzzle (or two, if you have the time) to make. Another way is to cut out the puzzle cards and paste each one on a 3" × 5" index card. There is a complete set of puzzle cards on pages 116–118. You may have to color code the difficulty levels on the cards for easy grouping. Before making any puzzles, hand each student a card and ask them to review it and decide if it contains a puzzle that they want to make. Give them five minutes to trade cards within the group or in the class if necessary.

Mathematical Exploration Activities

Activities 4 through 12 are designed to help students understand the mathematical principles underlying the puzzles and to guide their mathematical explorations. It is better to use these activities after the introduction to the related topics. Activity 5 requires no mathematical background, and Activity 4 and 6 each require a basic understanding of the mathematical properties of the puzzles components. Activities 7 through 12 are more advanced and require some understanding of the mathematical principles of the puzzles. In addition, Activity 7 requires a familiarity with graph representations and Activity 12 requires the application of mathematical functions.

Except for Activity 5—*Soma Cube* Constructions, the exploration activities do not require physical models of the puzzles or their components. However, it works better when physical models are used in these activities. Students can first make the puzzles and then explore the mathematic principles that apply.

Exploring Math Through Puzzles

Activity 1 — Puzzlers' Workshop (Easy)

Let's make puzzles! The following is a set of 15 cards showing puzzles selected for beginners or young puzzle-makers. The puzzles are easy to make but not necessarily easy to solve. Each card contains a picture of the puzzle, indicates the level of difficulty in construction, and lists the materials and tools needed for making the puzzle. Choose the puzzles that you want to make, collect all the materials and tools you'll need, and follow the puzzle instructions in this book.

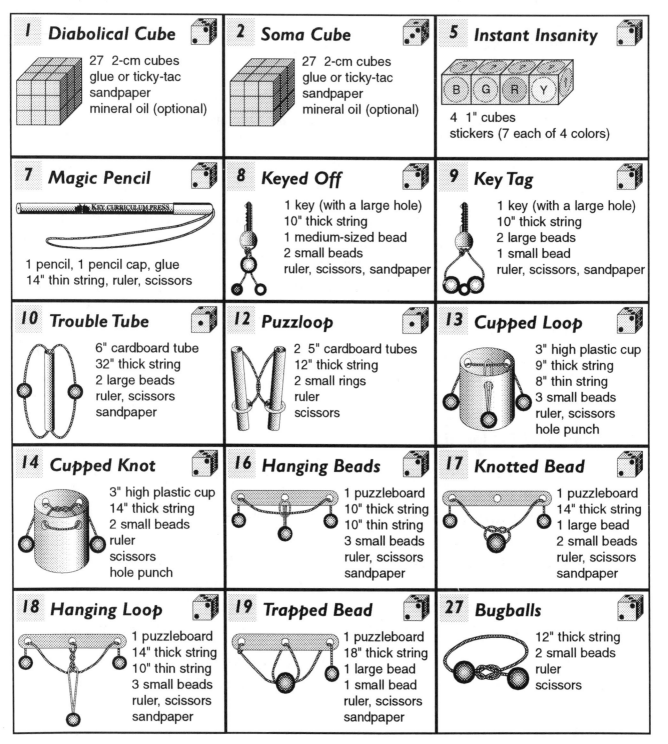

1 Diabolical Cube
27 2-cm cubes
glue or ticky-tac
sandpaper
mineral oil (optional)

2 Soma Cube
27 2-cm cubes
glue or ticky-tac
sandpaper
mineral oil (optional)

5 Instant Insanity
B G R Y
4 1" cubes
stickers (7 each of 4 colors)

7 Magic Pencil
KEY CURRICULUM PRESS.
1 pencil, 1 pencil cap, glue
14" thin string, ruler, scissors

8 Keyed Off
1 key (with a large hole)
10" thick string
1 medium-sized bead
2 small beads
ruler, scissors, sandpaper

9 Key Tag
1 key (with a large hole)
10" thick string
2 large beads
1 small bead
ruler, scissors, sandpaper

10 Trouble Tube
6" cardboard tube
32" thick string
2 large beads
ruler, scissors
sandpaper

12 Puzzloop
2 5" cardboard tubes
12" thick string
2 small rings
ruler
scissors

13 Cupped Loop
3" high plastic cup
9" thick string
8" thin string
3 small beads
ruler, scissors
hole punch

14 Cupped Knot
3" high plastic cup
14" thick string
2 small beads
ruler
scissors
hole punch

16 Hanging Beads
1 puzzleboard
10" thick string
10" thin string
3 small beads
ruler, scissors
sandpaper

17 Knotted Bead
1 puzzleboard
14" thick string
1 large bead
2 small beads
ruler, scissors
sandpaper

18 Hanging Loop
1 puzzleboard
14" thick string
10" thin string
3 small beads
ruler, scissors
sandpaper

19 Trapped Bead
1 puzzleboard
18" thick string
1 large bead
1 small bead
ruler, scissors
sandpaper

27 Bugballs
12" thick string
2 small beads
ruler
scissors

Activity 2 — Puzzlers' Workshop (Moderate)

Let's make puzzles! The following is a set of 15 cards showing puzzles selected for puzzle-makers with some experience. About half of the puzzles involve the use of wire, which requires some skill and practice. Each card contains a picture of the puzzle, indicates the level of difficulty in construction, and lists the materials and tools needed for making the puzzle. Choose the puzzles that you want to make, collect all the materials and tools you'll need, and follow the puzzle instructions in this book.

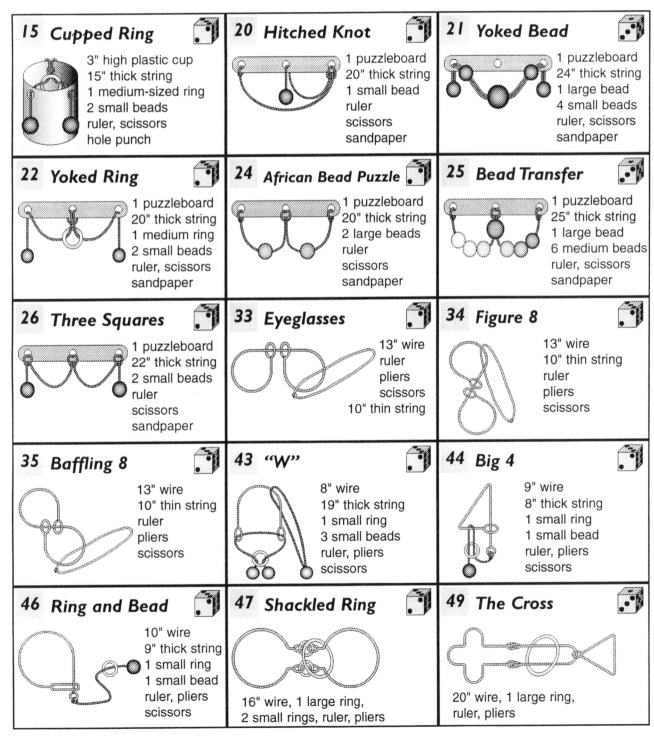

15 Cupped Ring

3" high plastic cup
15" thick string
1 medium-sized ring
2 small beads
ruler, scissors
hole punch

20 Hitched Knot

1 puzzleboard
20" thick string
1 small bead
ruler
scissors
sandpaper

21 Yoked Bead

1 puzzleboard
24" thick string
1 large bead
4 small beads
ruler, scissors
sandpaper

22 Yoked Ring

1 puzzleboard
20" thick string
1 medium ring
2 small beads
ruler, scissors
sandpaper

24 African Bead Puzzle

1 puzzleboard
20" thick string
2 large beads
ruler
scissors
sandpaper

25 Bead Transfer

1 puzzleboard
25" thick string
1 large bead
6 medium beads
ruler, scissors
sandpaper

26 Three Squares

1 puzzleboard
22" thick string
2 small beads
ruler
scissors
sandpaper

33 Eyeglasses

13" wire
ruler
pliers
scissors
10" thin string

34 Figure 8

13" wire
10" thin string
ruler
pliers
scissors

35 Baffling 8

13" wire
10" thin string
ruler
pliers
scissors

43 "W"

8" wire
19" thick string
1 small ring
3 small beads
ruler, pliers
scissors

44 Big 4

9" wire
8" thick string
1 small ring
1 small bead
ruler, pliers
scissors

46 Ring and Bead

10" wire
9" thick string
1 small ring
1 small bead
ruler, pliers
scissors

47 Shackled Ring

16" wire, 1 large ring,
2 small rings, ruler, pliers

49 The Cross

20" wire, 1 large ring,
ruler, pliers

Activity 3 — Puzzlers' Workshop (Hard)

Let's make puzzles! The following is a set of 15 cards showing puzzles selected for experienced puzzle-makers and those who are good at using pliers. The wire puzzles are the most challenging in this book. Even though they are hard to make, some of them are fairly easy to solve. Each card contains a picture of the puzzle, indicates the level of difficulty in construction, and lists the materials and tools needed for making the puzzle. Choose the puzzles that you want to make, collect all the materials and tools you'll need, and follow the puzzle instructions in this book.

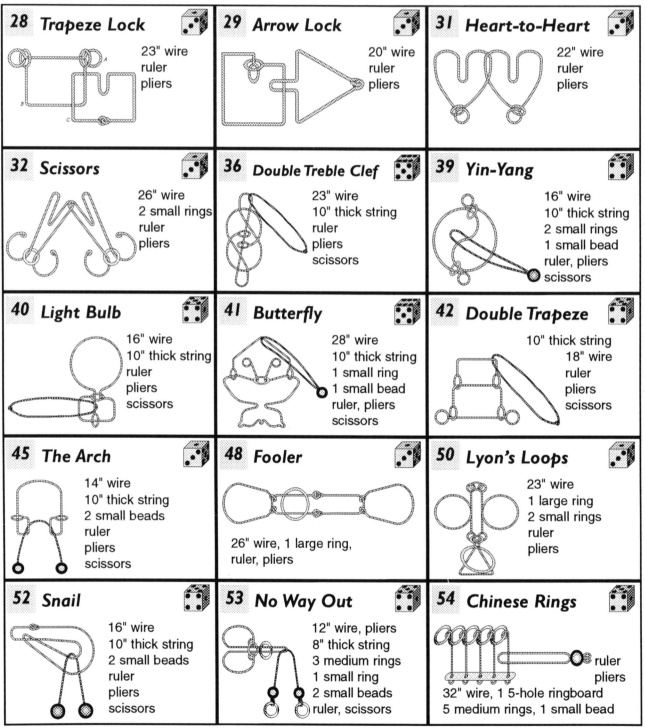

28 Trapeze Lock
23" wire
ruler
pliers

29 Arrow Lock
20" wire
ruler
pliers

31 Heart-to-Heart
22" wire
ruler
pliers

32 Scissors
26" wire
2 small rings
ruler
pliers

36 Double Treble Clef
23" wire
10" thick string
ruler
pliers
scissors

39 Yin-Yang
16" wire
10" thick string
2 small rings
1 small bead
ruler, pliers
scissors

40 Light Bulb
16" wire
10" thick string
ruler
pliers
scissors

41 Butterfly
28" wire
10" thick string
1 small ring
1 small bead
ruler, pliers
scissors

42 Double Trapeze
10" thick string
18" wire
ruler
pliers
scissors

45 The Arch
14" wire
10" thick string
2 small beads
ruler
pliers
scissors

48 Fooler
26" wire, 1 large ring,
ruler, pliers

50 Lyon's Loops
23" wire
1 large ring
2 small rings
ruler
pliers

52 Snail
16" wire
10" thick string
2 small beads
ruler
pliers
scissors

53 No Way Out
12" wire, pliers
8" thick string
3 medium rings
1 small ring
2 small beads
ruler, scissors

54 Chinese Rings
ruler
pliers
32" wire, 1 5-hole ringboard
5 medium rings, 1 small bead

Activity 4 — Polycubes

A **polycube** is a construction made of unit cubes put together face to face. Below is a collection of polycube figures of four cubes and five cubes. For easy reference, each figure is labeled with a letter.

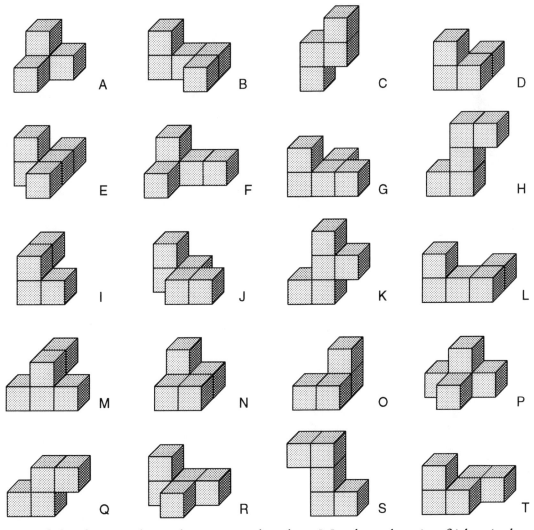

1. Some of the figures show the same polycubes. Match each pair of identical polycubes.
2. For each polycube pair you find, write a sequence of "left, right, clockwise, counter-clockwise" rotations to transform one polycube figure into the other. The rotations "left" and "right" indicate a 90° turn to the left or right around the top of a polycube piece, while the rotations "clockwise" and "counter-clockwise" indicate a 90° turn clockwise or counter-clockwise around the front of a polycube.
3. Identify each polycube that has reflexive symmetry.
4. For each reflexively symmetric polycube, sketch its plane(s) of symmetry.
5. For each nonreflexively symmetric polycube, find its mirror-image twin among the figures above.

Exploring Math Through Puzzles

Activity 5 — Soma Cube Constructions

Soma Cube is a very good puzzle, because in addition to the 240 different ways of putting the *Soma Cube* polycubes together to form a 3 × 3 × 3 cube, we can use all of the seven polycubes to make interesting constructions. Let's make these polycube pieces and use them for the following constructions.

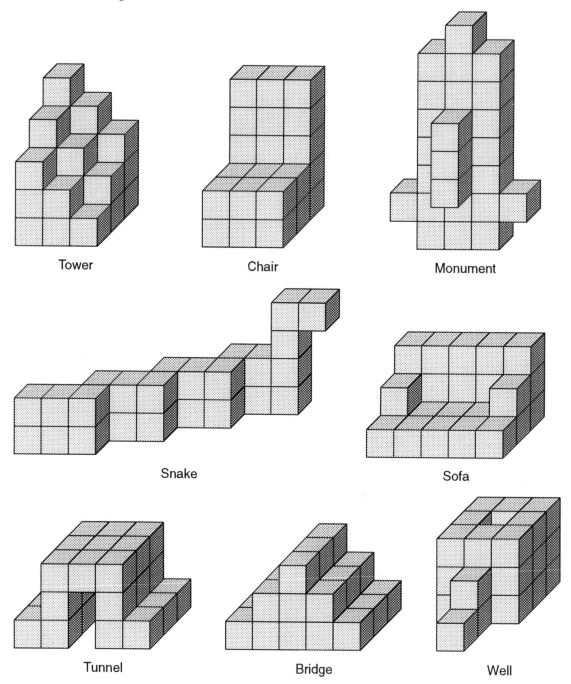

Tower   Chair   Monument

Snake   Sofa

Tunnel   Bridge   Well

Can you make some original constructions using all seven *Soma* polycubes? If so, sketch your original constructions.

Activity 6 — Describing a Cube

A cube with a different color on each of its six faces can be described in 24 different ways on †-shaped layouts. The first color layout below shows the first cube in the *Bewitching Cubes* puzzle. The second color layout shows the same cube rotated 90° clockwise around the top face. See if you can systematically color the rest of the layouts for this cube. The six colors are <u>R</u>ed, <u>B</u>lue, <u>G</u>reen, <u>Y</u>ellow, <u>O</u>range, and <u>L</u>ight Blue.

Exploring Math Through Puzzles

Activity 7 — Graph Representations

1. The graphs on the left and in the center represent the two sets of opposite-faced sides of four cubes arranged in a row. The graph on the right shows the six faces of a cube in a t-shaped layout. Using the graph on the left to represent the row's top and bottom sides and the graph in the center to represent the front and back sides, "color" the four cubes in the t-shaped layouts below. Don't worry about the colors on the side faces. Does this puzzle have a solution? Why or why not?

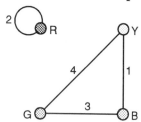

top and bottom opposite faces

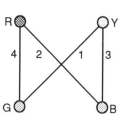

front and back opposite faces

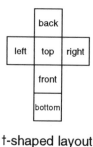

t-shaped layout

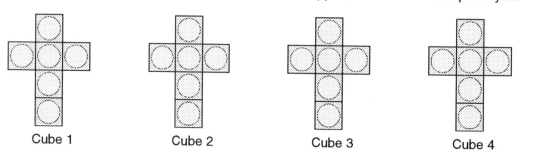

Cube 1   Cube 2   Cube 3   Cube 4

2. Use a graph representation to design a new puzzle with four cubes. Each cube in this puzzle has all four colors on its six faces. This puzzle is an *impossible* puzzle because there is no way that the four cubes can be arranged in a row so that all four colors show on each of the row's four sides.

First construct a 12-edge graph using the four colors as nodes. Your graph should show all the opposite-faced pairs of the four cubes. Then "color" the four cubes below.

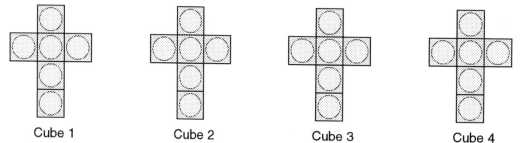

Cube 1   Cube 2   Cube 3   Cube 4

Activity 8 — Untangling Knots

A knot in daily life is just a tangled-up piece of string or rope with two loose ends. When a knot is tied with the help of another rigid object, such as a ring, we say it is **hitched** on that object. In a knot, the string **crosses** itself or the object it is hitched on. To untie such a knot, we can take one loose end and undo the **crossings** until there are no crossings left.

We all have some experience untying knots, and if we are patient enough, we can untie any knot. Puzzles based on tying and untying knots are called **untangling** puzzles. The following are three of the untangling puzzles in this book.

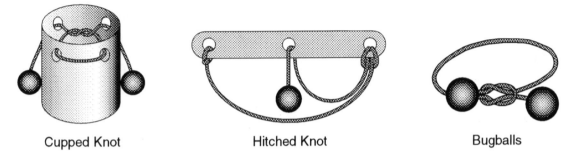

| Cupped Knot | Hitched Knot | Bugballs |

1. The objective of each puzzle is to untie the knot. Guess how each puzzle looks when the knot is untied, and make a drawing or sketch of the untangled puzzle.
2. Describe how to solve each puzzle.
3. After each puzzle is solved, can you tie the knot again, re-creating its initial state? Describe how you retie the knot of each puzzle.

Some untangling puzzles may not have untying a knot as their stated objective. The objective of *Keyed Off*, shown below, is to take the key off the string, while the objective of *Yoked Ring* is to remove the ring. However, in order to solve each puzzle, the knot hitched to the key or the puzzleboard has to be untied.

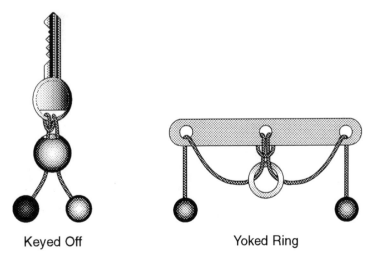

Keyed Off   Yoked Ring

4. Describe how you solve each puzzle and sketch how it looks when it is solved.

Exploring Math Through Puzzles

Activity 9 — Topological Transformations

When we look at an object topologically, we imagine that it can be stretched or twisted at will, and we focus mainly on the number of holes in the object. For example, there is no difference between a coffee cup and a doughnut, topologically speaking. If the coffee cup were made of soft rubber, we could smooth it into the shape of a doughnut by transforming the hole of the handle into the hole of the doughnut.

Obtaining one object from another through a series of such deformations is called **topological transformation**. Understanding how topological transformations work can help you reduce a complex structure into a simple one when solving puzzles.

For example, the puzzles *Double Treble Clef* and *Figure 8* appear to be structurally different, but they are, nevertheless, topologically equivalent. The following series of figures shows how the structure of *Double Treble Clef* can be topologically transformed into that of *Figure 8*.

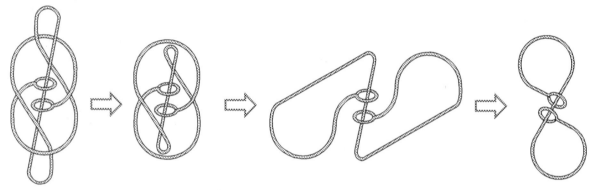

1. Describe the changes between the deformations.
2. If you know how to solve the puzzle *Figure 8* when a string loop is locked inside one of the large open loops, describe how to solve *Double Treble Clef.*

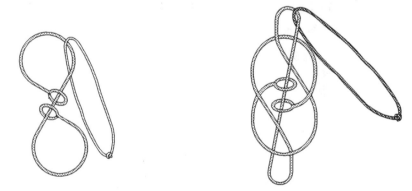

3. Sketch on the structure of *Figure 8* the point where string loop is out of the open loops. Is the string loop also free from the puzzle?
4. Sketch on the structure of *Double Treble Clef* the point where the string loop is out of the open loops. Is the string loop also free from the puzzle then? If not, what is in the way, and how can you free the string loop from the puzzle?

Activity 10 — Topological Difference

Some puzzles can appear very much alike, and yet they are topologically different from each other. The following are pairs of such puzzles.

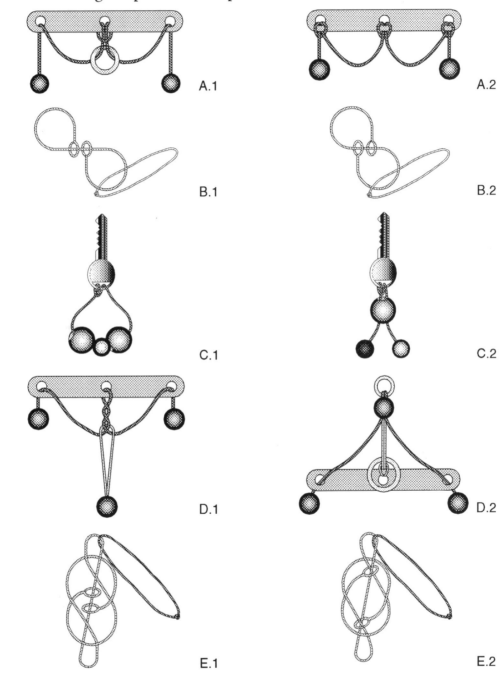

1. Describe the structural and topological differences between each pair of puzzles. Show the key differences that make the two puzzles different.
2. Identify the difference in the principles and objectives for each pair of puzzles.
3. Can you solve the puzzles? Describe how to solve each of the puzzles.

Activity 11 — Topological Equivalence

Two puzzles are **topologically equivalent** if one can be transformed into another through some deformations. Sometimes topologically equivalent puzzles are very different in their material and appearance. The following are some topological puzzles; each is labeled with a letter for easy reference.

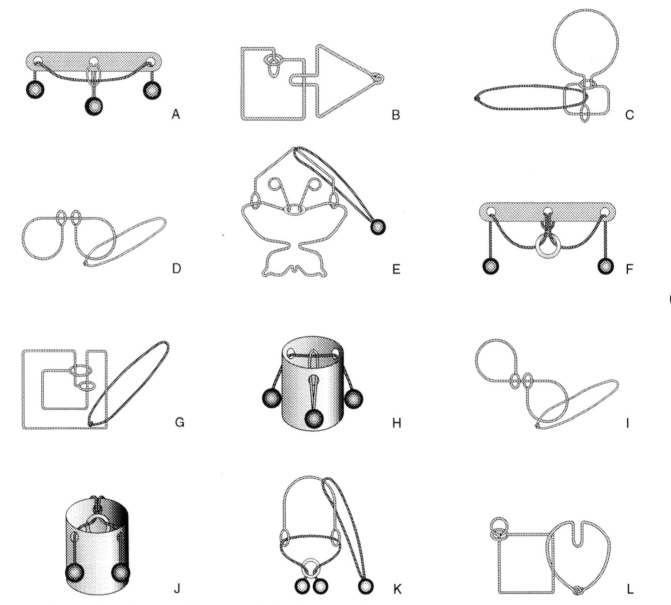

1. Guess the objective for each of the above puzzles.
2. Group the puzzles into topologically equivalent pairs.
3. For each pair of topologically equivalent puzzles, describe how one puzzle can be transformed into the other. Sketch the deformations if necessary.
4. Can you solve the puzzles? Describe how you solve each puzzle.

Activity 12 — Math with the Chinese Rings

Chinese Rings is a puzzle of nested open loops. The rings in the puzzle are numbered from left to right with numbers 1 to *n*, where 1 is the outermost and *n* is the innermost ring. In the puzzle's initial state, the handle is often locked inside the loop formed with the innermost (rightmost) ring, as shown above in the five-ring version of the puzzle. The objective of the puzzle is to free the handle from the puzzle.

The function *Moves(n)* computes the number of moves needed either to free the handle from the *n*th ring or to lock it into the loop by the *n*th ring.

$$Moves(n) = \begin{cases} 1 & \text{if } n = 1 \\ Moves(n-1) + 1 + Moves(n-1) = 2 \times Moves(n-1) + 1 & \text{if } n > 1 \end{cases}$$

1. Use the function *Moves(n)* to compute the following:
   a. Moves(1) =
   b. Moves(2) =
   c. Moves(3) =
   d. Moves(4) =

2. What's the relationship between *Moves(n)* and *Moves(n+1)*?

3. The above *Moves(n)* function is **recursive** because the function is used in the definition of itself. Can you write a **nonrecursive** function *NewMoves(n)* that gives the same results as *Moves(n)*?

4. If you could make one move per second when solving a *Chinese Rings* puzzle, how long would it take you to solve the *Chinese Rings* puzzle with 1, 2, 3, ... up to 32 rings? Fill in your calculations below.

Number of rings	years	days	hours	minutes	seconds
1	—	—	—	—	1
2	—	—	—	—	3
3	—	—	—	—	—
4	—	—	—	—	—
5	—	—	—	—	—
10	—	—	—	—	—
15	—	—	—	—	—
20	—	—	—	—	—
25	—	—	—	—	—
30	—	—	—	—	—
31	—	—	—	—	—
32	—	—	—	—	—

5. What do you think the maximum number of rings in a *Chinese Rings* puzzle should be? Why?

6. How many rings would you prefer to have in your own *Chinese Rings* puzzle? Why?

Appendix A — Puzzle Materials and Tools

Following is a list of all the materials and tools needed to make the 54 puzzles in this book.

Materials	Quantity	Specifications/Preference
Puzzleboards	11	6" × 3/4" board with three 1/4" holes
Chinese Rings board	1	5" × 1/2" board with five 3/16" holes
Large cubes	10	1" size, wood
Small cubes	108	2 cm size, wood, only need 27 if reusing
Large rings	6	1 1/2" outside dia., 1 1/16" inside dia.
Medium-sized rings	10	1 1/8" outside dia., 1 3/16" inside dia.
Small rings	18	3/4" outside dia., 9/16" inside dia.
Large beads	10	15/16" dia., with 5/16" dia. hole
Medium-sized beads	9	13/16" dia., with 5/16" dia. hole
Small beads	47	11/16" dia., with 1/8" dia. hole
Thick string	42'	1/8" dia., braided nylon
Thin string	8'	3/32" dia., braided nylon
Wire	44'	14-gauge, galvanized
Pencil	1	full-length (7"), round
Pencil cap	1	metal, with a small hole at the end
Stickers in 4 colors	28	7 stickers in each color
Stickers in 6 colors	36	6 stickers in each color
Old keys	2	with holes at least 1/4" in diameter
Paper cup or plastic bottle	3	3" high and 2" in diameter
Cardboard tubes	5	6" long, from pants hanger

Tools	Quantity	Specifications
Ruler	1	12" long
Scissors	1	
Long-nosed pliers	1	at least 6" size
Wood glue	2 oz.	to permanently join cubes
Ticky-tac	1 oz.	to temporarily join cubes
Sandpaper	2 sheets	150 or 180-grain, 4 1/2" × 5 1/2"
Lighter	1	for sealing the string ends
Candle	1	for sealing the string ends
Plastic-coated twist-tie	1	4" long, for making a threading aid

Appendix B — Finding the Materials

Appendix A lists all the materials needed to make all 54 puzzles introduced in this book. If you decide to make some of the puzzles, and I do hope you do, then you'll face the problem of finding the materials. Where can you find all the materials?

Ordering a Puzzle Kit from Key Curriculum Press

Key Curriculum Press has designed a Puzzle Kit to accompany this book. The kit contains most of the materials you'll need to make all 54 puzzles in this book. All you need to find is the wire, some common household items, and the tools. For more information, please contact Key Curriculum Press by phone at 1-800-995-MATH or by mail at 1150 65th Street, Emeryville, California 94608.

Local Hardware and Crafts Stores

Your local hardware and crafts stores sell most of the materials and tools needed for making the puzzles. In fact, I bought most of my materials and tools from these stores when developing the prototypes of the puzzles.

Around the House

Try to be resourceful! Surely there are some things in the house that can be used to make puzzles. For example, big buttons can generally be used as substitutes for beads. Common household items can also be substituted for some of the other materials. Here is a list:

Materials	Substitutes	Comments
Puzzleboards	tongue depressors	drill holes in them
	cardboard cut-outs	easy to make, not as strong
Large cubes	folded paper	can make them larger than 1" size
Rings	key rings, keys, washers	holes have to be large enough
Beads	large buttons, keys	hard to hide knots inside holes
String	knitting yarn	doesn't last as long, hard to seal ends
Wire	coat hangers	harder to bend, but costs nothing

Appendix C — Need a Hint?

As you can see, we are not offering any straightforward solutions to the puzzles presented in this book. However, plenty of hints are given for each type of puzzle in the section "The Mathematics of Puzzles." Following is a list of the 54 puzzles with information on their levels of difficulty, the mathematical principles involved, and hints on how to solve them.

#	Name of Puzzle	Make	Solve	Principle	Comments
1	Diabolical Cube	2	2	comb. geometry	13 solutions
2	Soma Cube	3	3	comb. geometry	240 solutions
3	Half-Hour Cube	3	4	comb. geometry	1 solution
4	Nob's Cube	3	5	comb. geometry	1 solution
5	Instant Insanity	2	4	object orientation	solved pp. 13–15
6	Bewitching Cubes	2	4	object orientation	refer to pp. 13–15
7	Magic Pencil	2	4	loop extension	solved pp. 29–31
8	Keyed Off	2	2	untying knot	refer to pp. 27–28
9	Key Tag	2	3	knot equivalence	solved pp. 25–26
10	Trouble Tube	1	1	knot equivalence	refer to pp. 25–26
11	Double the Trouble	1	2	knot equivalence	refer to pp. 25–26
12	Puzzloop	1	2	open loop	refer to pp. 16–18
13	Cupped Bead Loop	2	1	open loop	refer to pp. 16–18
14	Cupped Knot	2	2	untying knot	refer to pp. 27–28
15	Cupped Ring	2	3	untying knot	refer to pp. 27–28
16	Hanging Beads	2	1	open loop	refer to pp. 16–18
17	Knotted Bead	2	2	untying knot	refer to pp. 27–28
18	Hanging Loop	2	2	open loop	refer to pp. 16–18
19	Trapped Bead	2	2	untying knot	refer to pp. 27–28
20	Hitched Knot	2	3	untying knot	solved pp. 27–28
21	Yoked Bead	3	3	loop extension	refer to pp. 29–31
22	Yoked Ring	2	3	untying knot	refer to pp. 27–28
23	Hanging Ring	3	3	untying knot	refer to pp. 27–28
24	African Bead Puzzle	2	3	knot equivalence	refer to pp. 25–26
25	Bead Transfer	3	4	knot equivalence	refer to pp. 25–26

#	Name of Puzzle	Make/Solve		Principle	Comments
26	Three Squares	2	3	untying knot	refer to pp. 27–28
27	Bugballs	2	3	untying knot	refer to pp. 27–28
28	Trapeze Lock	3	2	open loop	refer to pp. 16–18
29	Arrow Lock	3	2	open loop	refer to pp. 16–18
30	Double Crossed	4	3	open loop	refer to pp. 16–18
31	Heart-to-Heart	3	2	open loop	refer to pp. 16–18
32	Scissors	3	2	open loop	refer to pp. 16–18
33	Eyeglasses	2	2	open loop	refer to pp. 16–18
34	Figure 8	2	2	open loop	refer to pp. 16–18
35	Baffling 8	2	3	?	can you solve it?
36	Double Treble Clef	5	3	open loop	refer to pp. 16–19
37	Straight Clef	5	2	open loop	refer to pp. 16–19
38	Trouble Clef	5	3	open loop	refer to pp. 16–19
39	Yin-Yang	4	2	open loop	refer to pp. 16–18
40	Light Bulb	4	3	open loop, nested	refer to pp. 16–20
41	Butterfly	5	3	open loop, nested	refer to pp. 16–20
42	Double Trapeze	4	3	open loop, nested	solved pp. 19–20
43	"W"	2	3	open loop, nested	refer to pp. 16–20
44	Big 4	2	3	untying knot	refer to pp. 27–28
45	The Arch	3	4	untying knot	refer to pp. 27–28
46	Ring and Bead	2	3	unclassified	you are on your own
47	Shackled Ring	3	2	folding & twisting	solved pp. 32–33
48	Fooler	3	3	folding & twisting	refer to pp. 32–33
49	The Cross	3	2	folding & twisting	refer to pp. 32–33
50	Lyon's Loops	3	3	folding & twisting	refer to pp. 32–33
51	Triangular Trickery	3	3	folding & twisting	refer to pp. 32–33
52	Snail	4	4	unclassified	solved pp. 34–35
53	No Way Out	4	3	unclassified	solved p. 36
54	Chinese Rings	4	5	open loop, nested	solved pp. 16–24

Exploring Math Through Puzzles

Puzzle Index Cards (1 - 18)

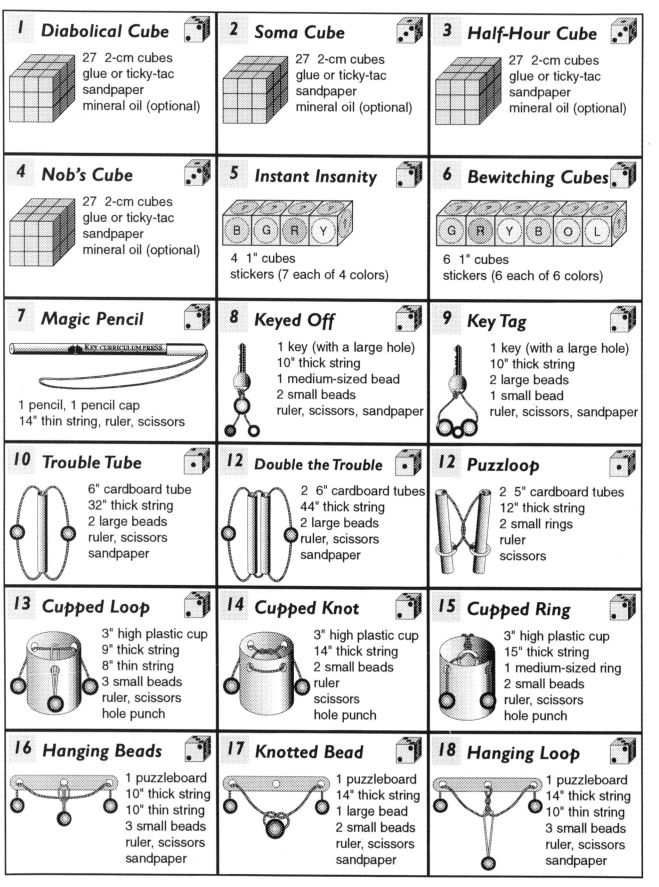

1 Diabolical Cube
27 2-cm cubes
glue or ticky-tac
sandpaper
mineral oil (optional)

2 Soma Cube
27 2-cm cubes
glue or ticky-tac
sandpaper
mineral oil (optional)

3 Half-Hour Cube
27 2-cm cubes
glue or ticky-tac
sandpaper
mineral oil (optional)

4 Nob's Cube
27 2-cm cubes
glue or ticky-tac
sandpaper
mineral oil (optional)

5 Instant Insanity
B G R Y
4 1" cubes
stickers (7 each of 4 colors)

6 Bewitching Cubes
G R Y B O L
6 1" cubes
stickers (6 each of 6 colors)

7 Magic Pencil
KEY CURRICULUM PRESS
1 pencil, 1 pencil cap
14" thin string, ruler, scissors

8 Keyed Off
1 key (with a large hole)
10" thick string
1 medium-sized bead
2 small beads
ruler, scissors, sandpaper

9 Key Tag
1 key (with a large hole)
10" thick string
2 large beads
1 small bead
ruler, scissors, sandpaper

10 Trouble Tube
6" cardboard tube
32" thick string
2 large beads
ruler, scissors
sandpaper

12 Double the Trouble
2 6" cardboard tubes
44" thick string
2 large beads
ruler, scissors
sandpaper

12 Puzzloop
2 5" cardboard tubes
12" thick string
2 small rings
ruler
scissors

13 Cupped Loop
3" high plastic cup
9" thick string
8" thin string
3 small beads
ruler, scissors
hole punch

14 Cupped Knot
3" high plastic cup
14" thick string
2 small beads
ruler
scissors
hole punch

15 Cupped Ring
3" high plastic cup
15" thick string
1 medium-sized ring
2 small beads
ruler, scissors
hole punch

16 Hanging Beads
1 puzzleboard
10" thick string
10" thin string
3 small beads
ruler, scissors
sandpaper

17 Knotted Bead
1 puzzleboard
14" thick string
1 large bead
2 small beads
ruler, scissors
sandpaper

18 Hanging Loop
1 puzzleboard
14" thick string
10" thin string
3 small beads
ruler, scissors
sandpaper

Puzzle Index Cards (19 - 36)

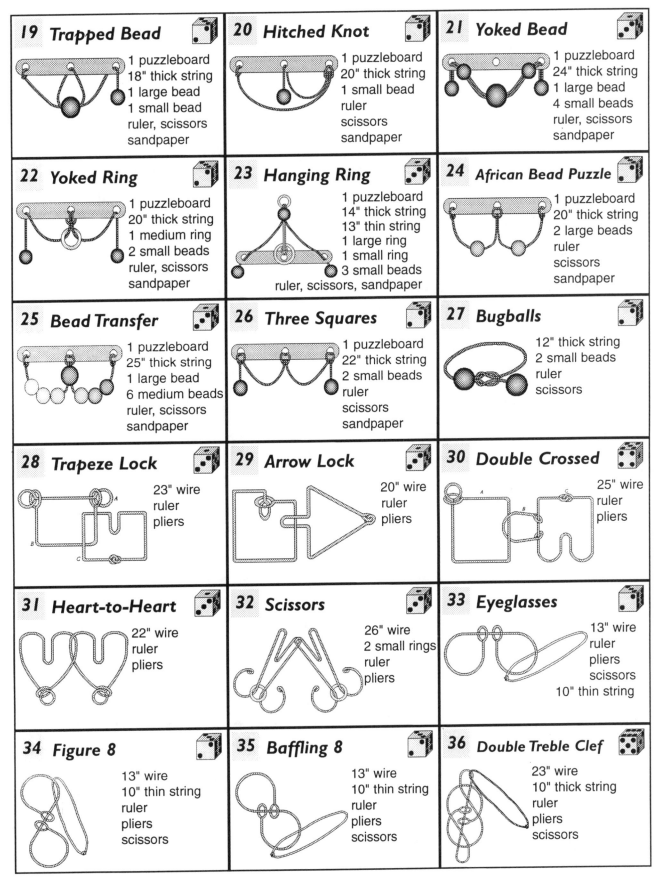

19 Trapped Bead

1 puzzleboard
18" thick string
1 large bead
1 small bead
ruler, scissors
sandpaper

20 Hitched Knot

1 puzzleboard
20" thick string
1 small bead
ruler
scissors
sandpaper

21 Yoked Bead

1 puzzleboard
24" thick string
1 large bead
4 small beads
ruler, scissors
sandpaper

22 Yoked Ring

1 puzzleboard
20" thick string
1 medium ring
2 small beads
ruler, scissors
sandpaper

23 Hanging Ring

1 puzzleboard
14" thick string
13" thin string
1 large ring
1 small ring
3 small beads
ruler, scissors, sandpaper

24 African Bead Puzzle

1 puzzleboard
20" thick string
2 large beads
ruler
scissors
sandpaper

25 Bead Transfer

1 puzzleboard
25" thick string
1 large bead
6 medium beads
ruler, scissors
sandpaper

26 Three Squares

1 puzzleboard
22" thick string
2 small beads
ruler
scissors
sandpaper

27 Bugballs

12" thick string
2 small beads
ruler
scissors

28 Trapeze Lock

23" wire
ruler
pliers

29 Arrow Lock

20" wire
ruler
pliers

30 Double Crossed

25" wire
ruler
pliers

31 Heart-to-Heart

22" wire
ruler
pliers

32 Scissors

26" wire
2 small rings
ruler
pliers

33 Eyeglasses

13" wire
ruler
pliers
scissors
10" thin string

34 Figure 8

13" wire
10" thin string
ruler
pliers
scissors

35 Baffling 8

13" wire
10" thin string
ruler
pliers
scissors

36 Double Treble Clef

23" wire
10" thick string
ruler
pliers
scissors

Puzzle Index Cards (37 - 54)

37 Straight Clef
23" wire
10" thick string
ruler
pliers
scissors

38 Trouble Clef
23" wire
10" thick string
ruler
pliers
scissors

39 Yin-Yang
16" wire
10" thick string
2 small rings
1 small bead
ruler, pliers
scissors

40 Light Bulb
16" wire
10" thick string
ruler
pliers
scissors

41 Butterfly
28" wire
10" thick string
1 small ring
1 small bead
ruler, pliers
scissors

42 Double Trapeze
10" thick string
18" wire
ruler
pliers
scissors

43 "W"
8" wire
19" thick string
1 small ring
3 small beads
ruler, pliers
scissors

44 Big 4
9" wire
8" thick string
1 small ring
1 small bead
ruler, pliers
scissors

45 The Arch
14" wire
10" thick string
2 small beads
ruler
pliers
scissors

46 Ring and Bead
10" wire
9" thick string
1 small ring
1 small bead
ruler, pliers
scissors

47 Shackled Ring
16" wire, 1 large ring,
2 small rings, ruler, pliers

48 Fooler
26" wire, 1 large ring,
ruler, pliers

49 The Cross
20" wire, 1 large ring,
ruler, pliers

50 Lyon's Loops
23" wire
1 large ring
2 small rings
ruler
pliers

51 Triangular Trickery
35" wire
1 large ring
2 small rings
ruler
pliers

52 Snail
16" wire
10" thick string
2 small beads
ruler
pliers
scissors

53 No Way Out
12" wire
8" thick string
3 medium rings
1 small ring
2 small beads, ruler
pliers, scissors

54 Chinese Rings
32" wire
ruler
pliers
1 5-hole ringboard
5 medium rings, 1 small bead

118   *Exploring Math Through Puzzles*

Bibliography

Adams, Colin C. *The Knot Book: An Elementary Introduction to the Mathematical Theory of Knots.* W. H. Freeman and Company, New York, 1994.

Barr, Stephen. *Experiments in Topology.* Dover Publications, New York, 1964.

Béart, Charles. *Jeux et jouets de l'ouest africain, Volume 1.* L'Institut Francais d'Afrique Noire, Ifan Dakar, 1955.

Berlekamp, Elwyn, John H. Conway, and Richard Guy. *Winning Ways for Your Mathematical Plays, Volume 1: Games in General.* Academic Press, London, 1982.

———. *Winning Ways for Your Mathematical Plays, Volume 2: Games in Particular.* Academic Press, London, 1982.

Budworth, Geoffrey. *The Knot Book.* Sterling Publishing Company, New York, 1985.

Chartrand, Gary. *Introductory Graph Theory.* Dover Publications, New York, 1977

Coffin, Stewart T. *The Puzzling World of Polyhedral Dissections: Hundreds of 3-D Puzzles to Build and Solve.* Oxford University Press, New York, 1990.

Culin, Stewart. *Games of the Orient.* Charles E. Tuttle Company, Tokyo, 1958.

Dudeney, Henry E. *Amusements in Mathematics.* Dover Publications, New York, 1958.

Fawdry, Marguerite. *Chinese Childhood: A Miscellany of Mythology, Folklore, Fact and Fable.* Pollocks Toy Theatres Limited, London, 1977.

Filipiak, Anthony S. *Mathematical Puzzles and Other Brain Twisters: 100 Man Made Problems—How to Make and Solve Them.* Bell Publishing Company, New York, 1942.

Gardner, Martin. *Knotted Doughnuts and Other Mathematical Entertainments.* W. H. Freeman and Company, New York, 1986.

———. *Mathematical Carnival.* Alfred A. Knopf, New York, 1975.

———. *New Mathematical Diversions from Scientific American.* Simon & Schuster, New York, 1966.

———. *The Scientific American Book of Mathematical Puzzles & Diversions.* Simon & Schuster, New York, 1959.

———. *The Second Scientific American Book of Mathematical Puzzles & Diversions.* University of Chicago Press, Chicago, 1961.

———. *The Unexpected Hanging and Other Mathematical Diversions.* University of Chicago Press, Chicago, 1969.

Golomb, Solomon W. *Polyominoes: Puzzles, Patterns, Problems, and Packings*. Princeton University Press, Princeton, 1994.

Hoffmann, Louis. *Hoffmann's Puzzles Old and New*. L. E. Hordern, Reading, England, 1993

O'Beirne, T. H. *Puzzles & Paradoxes*. Oxford University Press, New York, 1965.

Slocum, Jerry and Jack Botermans. *The Book of Ingenious & Diabolical Puzzles*. Times Books, New York, 1994.

———. *New Book of Puzzles: 101 Classic and Modern Puzzles to Make and Solve*. W. H. Freeman and Company, New York, 1992.

———. *Puzzles Old and New: How to Make and Solve Them*. University of Washington Press, Seattle, 1986.

Steinhaus, H. *Mathematical Snapshots*. Oxford University Press, New York, 1960.

Van Delft, Pieter, and Jack Botermans. *Creative Puzzles of the World*. Key Curriculum Press, Berkeley, 1995

Wells, Kenneth. *Wooden Puzzles and Games: Intriguing Projects You Can Make*. Sterling Publishing Company, New York, 1983.

Wyatt, Edwin M. *Puzzles in Wood*. Woodcraft Supply Corporation, Parkersburg, WV, 1992.

Yoshigahara, Nob. *Puzzle in Wood*. Sowa Shuppan, Tokyo, 1987.

Yu, Chong-En. *Ingenious Ring Puzzle Book: Ancient Wisdom Game*. Shanghai Culture Publishing, Shanghai, 1958.